POSTER BOY

A MEMOIR OF ART AND POLITICS

PETER DREW

Black Inc.

Published by Black Inc.,
an imprint of Schwartz Publishing Pty Ltd
Level 1, 221 Drummond Street
Carlton VIC 3053, Australia
enquiries@blackincbooks.com
www.blackincbooks.com

9781760641337 (paperback)
9781743820841 (ebook)

 A catalogue record for this
book is available from the
National Library of Australia

Cover and text design by Akiko Chan
Typesetting by Dennis Grauel
All images © Peter Drew unless stated on p. 249
Author photograph by Rebecca Mansell
Part title and epilogue backgrounds: photographs by Cafe Racer / Shutterstock

Printed in Australia by McPherson's Printing Group.

For my parents and my brothers

PART ONE

REAL
AUSTRALIANS

Introduction

For the past five years I've stuck up thousands of posters across Australia in an effort to challenge and expand our national identity. It started with a focus on Australia's treatment of asylum seekers, but with each new poster design the project's scope has grown to encompass our broader national mythology. I've been rewarded with attention, accolades and praise.

Given my choice of occupation, you might expect that I have unshakable convictions about social justice and human rights, but I don't. I'm sometimes called an activist, but it's not a label I enjoy. I don't have a personal attachment to any particular cause or marginalised group. I don't even like political art. Given all this, why do what I do? That's the question I've been asking myself lately, with nagging persistence.

Sometimes journalists ask me the same question, and my answer is usually evasive and always inadequate. It gives me the strange feeling that I don't understand myself well enough for a man in his mid-thirties. The feeling grows when I consider the irony that my posters aim to confront the Australian people's collective lack of self-awareness. Maybe it's time that I cast out the beam in my own eye and made sense of my motivations.

Since I started sticking up my posters I've had countless confrontations with people on the street. They're almost always men, usually my dad's age and often angry. I wish I could say I've always behaved fairly towards them, but I haven't. I wish I could say I've never taunted these men and inflamed their insecurities, but I often have. Because men like that always have personal inadequacies hidden beneath the veil of their political convictions. I know this because I'm really no better than they are. I feel that I owe them an apology, or at least some acknowledgement that we're not so different.

The other group of people with whom my interactions follow a troubling pattern are the young political activists. These types have usually dedicated a whole semester to swallowing whatever worldview best weaponises their angst, before setting out to fix the world. Like budding Raskolnikovs, they're irritatingly intelligent. They hate my posters for their appeal to the political centre. They hate the ironies that seep between the cracks in their convictions. Like the puritans of old, they ultimately hate their own imperfectibility. I honestly admire their enthusiasm but it's a terrible thing to have a chip on a young shoulder. I should know.

Australia also has a chip on its shoulder. I've seen it everywhere I go with my posters. We hide it beneath our 'she'll be right' larrikinism and Anzac Day pageantry, while our true identity is deep and dark and personal. For the last 200 years Australia has been playing the role of Western civilisation's fun-loving sidekick. We like to see ourselves as the friendly underdog with heart. We lack the courage to take full responsibility for our history because our national psyche is adolescent. We won't admit that we traded innocence for power a long time ago. But our immaturity isn't entirely our fault; it's also due to a spiritual poverty that's afflicting the Western world at large.

I chose to be an artist rather than follow my training in psychology because art is really a spiritual project. Since the Enlightenment, art has become the Western world's attempt to remedy its spiritual disenchantment, especially during the twentieth century. The Cubists initiated a cult of abstraction while the Surrealists sought to replace God with the subconscious. The Dadaists, ahead of the game, answered the death-of-God by exulting in the absurd. One by one, every Modern Art movement collapsed under the weight of its own pomposity and the squeeze of free-market nihilism. Today we view art history through the lens of the market. As a result, we see only a succession of novelties rather than a battle of ideas. Many of today's artists have embraced the market's hunger for sheer novelty. Others have learnt to mimic the academic jargon of the curatorial clergy who run the state-sponsored art institutions and offer refuge to artists who mutter the correct incantations. Increasingly those mutterings favour ideology over aesthetic or spiritual aspirations. My posters are also a symptom of this trend. Without spiritual aspiration, political art is little more than a visual commentary on power. Artists like me have forgotten how to adapt and renew our most powerful unifying myths. It's no surprise that tribalism and stale ideology keep moving in to fill the vacuum.

This might all seem a little grim and abstract, so I'll try to bring it back home. I can describe my own spiritual poverty with a simple phrase: my struggle to 'become a man'. Of course the phrase is uncomfortably anachronistic, just like the phrase 'Real Australian'. It's a phrase that attracts suspicion, like a dog whistle to toxic tradition or a roadblock to the genderless utopia that forever waits beyond the horizon. But the type of manhood that interests me is about responsibility, not entitlement. In this sense, my art is a personal attempt to reform my own sense of manhood, by attempting to reform our collective sense of nationhood.

Just as Australia's psyche is adolescent, I too feel more like a boy than a man. I'd like to fix that. In this book I'm going to explore my strange journey to becoming a poster boy of hashtag activism. I'm going to be open about the personal shortcomings that motivated my projects. I'm going to be open about my mistakes, public and private. I'm going to be open about everything I've learnt from the people who have tried to stop me, and those who have helped. I'm going to tell you all this because it's what I need to do in order to grow. After thirty-five years, I'm tired of being a boy who lives in a childish country.

Ambition and Apologies

YOUR CHILDREN'S FUTURE IS A FANTASY

WHY?

ENERGY DEMANDS, WATER SHORTAGES + CLIMATE CHANGE

BUT THANKS FOR THE ROCK N ROLL

I made this stencil in October 2009. I'm not particularly proud of it. In fact, I find it pretty embarrassing, but I think it's worth showing you because it reveals something about me that still hasn't changed. It's also the first piece of street art I ever made.

I grew up in a household where no one ever apologised and no one was ever forgiven. I know that sounds a little dramatic but it's really not much of an exaggeration. It's taken me a long time to learn how to apologise and I'm still not very good at it. If you don't believe me, just ask my wife. Whenever we have an argument I turn into a Rubik's cube made of stone, only less emotional.

The atmosphere at home cycled between dormant, snarky and explosive. The root cause was definitely my parents' relationship. I've never witnessed an act of physical affection between them. Sometimes they bicker in an affectionate way but I've never seen them exchange a simple kiss or a hug. I didn't realise that my parents' relationship was unusual until I was twenty-one. I distinctly remember being at a friend's house and seeing my friend's parents casually give each other a kiss. I thought, *What the fuck was that?* I asked my friend about it and he looked at me like I was weird. Then it occurred to me that maybe I was weird. The exact reason for my parents' estrangement had always been a mystery, although I can't say I spent much time wondering about it. That's just the way it was.

Despite our family's lack of affection there was never any lack of ambition. In fact, there was so much emphasis placed upon achievement that I wondered whether one compensated for the other. When it came to encouraging good grades, my dad had a simple system: he gave me $20 every time I got an A. So I got straight As. I was making $120 every term and it was easy money. I wasn't particularly smart, I just didn't socialise. That's how I graduated from high school with an excellent Tertiary Entrance Rank and the social skills of a shut-in. I was perfectly qualified to follow my half-baked dream of becoming an accountant. The University of Adelaide offered me a position to study Commerce at its prestigious business school and my parents couldn't have been happier. Then, in the summer between school and uni, I discovered friends, drugs and girls. I dropped out of uni within a month.

Throughout that period I was quite happy to be a fuck-up. Subconsciously I'd realised that my parents' love was conditional upon my achievements, so I felt a perverse sense of righteousness in squandering my own potential. However, my cynicism wasn't reserved for my parents. I'd decided that the whole world was faulty and I was going to escape it by constantly getting high. My new lifestyle didn't sit well with my family, especially since I was still living at home. At one point the tension spilled over into violence. I was arguing with

Dad when a fight broke out between me and my older brother, Julian. My younger brother, Simon, jumped in to help me. Then Dad jumped on Simon. For a moment there were four grown men brawling in the hallway. It's funny to remember but it was bloody awful at the time. Afterwards my dad and I were both in tears and he told me that he loved me. That's when I knew I had to get my shit together.

Reluctantly, I enrolled in a course of Psychology and Philosophy. I wasn't interested in a career in either discipline but I did have a strong desire to understand the world. Really, I wanted to understand myself. During the course I gravitated towards art. I wasn't particularly talented, I just felt like I had something to say. And that's how I became an artist. I moved into a share house, fell in love and got married.

I was a painter before I got into street art. I painted large, colourful canvases that bear little resemblance to the art in this book. In 2008 I was offered my first solo exhibition at a small commercial gallery in Adelaide's eastern suburbs. The gallery owner believed my work was saleable, but that was before the global financial crisis. When my exhibition finally opened a year later, the art market had collapsed. I only sold a few paintings. The owner of the gallery said I was lucky to have sold anything.

I took my unsold paintings back to my studio. Before the exhibition I was actually scared to sell them, but now I was afraid I'd never get rid of them. I stacked them in the corner of my studio and covered them with a sheet, but I couldn't ignore them. Every time I sat down to paint new work, there they were, mocking my ambition. I began to wonder whether I should quit.

I'm not sure 'ambition' is the right word for the way I feel about art. When you're a kid you don't have ambition; you have a 'dream'.

We dream of growing up and doing something good, because we're encouraged to believe that the world is good. We're encouraged to believe that there's a place waiting for us in the world. For me, ever since crossing the threshold into adulthood I've had the nagging feeling that the world wasn't worth taking seriously. That I didn't really want to participate. I was happy to observe life from the outside, but becoming a part of the world wasn't for me. I didn't know where that feeling came from but I believed that art was my best hope for fighting a way out of it.

So I really couldn't quit. I needed to keep making art but I had to find some form of expression that didn't rely on the disposable income of art collectors. It just so happened that my housemate was a street artist. At night he would go out to paint walls in the city. I kept asking him questions about how he did it, so one night he offered to take me out and show me the ropes. It was exactly what I needed. When you're sneaking around the city at night you feel like a kid again. The seriousness of the world is unmasked as a series of façades, dead objects just waiting to be painted. I was immediately hooked. Out on the street I could say anything I wanted. So what did I want to say?

The idea for my first stencil came to me one night while painting in my studio. I was listening to the pithy pessimism of Radio National's 'Late Night Live'. Phillip Adams' guest was predicting a future of terminal decline but instead of being worried, I felt emboldened. Alone in my studio, I listened intently, nurturing my wounded sense of entitlement as I designed my stencil on the computer my parents had bought for me. I used an old projector I'd stolen from the University of Adelaide to transfer the design to a large piece of cardboard. With a $2 Stanley knife, I cut out each letter. From beginning to end it took less than an hour. Finally, I picked up my $3 can of black spray-paint and headed out into the night. I was ready to deploy my 26-year-old wisdom. I was ready to become a street artist. I kept painting and holding exhibitions for another two years, but it was only a matter of time before street art took over my life.

Twenty-six is pretty late to begin a career in vandalism. While many graffiti artists are hanging up their spurs at that age, I was just getting started. Since then I've become both better and worse. My posters have become more optimistic but there's still something aggressive and arrogant in the way I stick them up on other people's property. I can offer various intellectual arguments for my behaviour but the real reason is temperamental. Part of me would rather be in the position of owing an apology than asking for approval. After almost ten years of making street art, that still hasn't changed.

Finding Out

My life began to make more sense, at least to me, on the day I ruined my parents' car.

It was a clear autumn day in 2011. I'd borrowed their Toyota Corolla to pick up a 15-litre can of paint for a wall I was planning to hit that night. I was going through a stage of doing 'rollers', a type of graffiti where you use a paint roller and extension pole to write enormous letters, often two storeys high. My favourite trick was to enter abandoned buildings and use the roof access to paint over the side of the building. Maximum risk, maximum reward. It's the sort of thing you need to psych yourself up for and plan out in steps. At the time I was locked in competition with another graffiti artist. We'd had a falling out and everybody knew about it, so the battle was on for dominance of the Adelaide street art scene. Deep down we both knew it was silly but we were still 100 per cent committed to crushing our opponent. Such is the mentality of males in their late twenties with unresolved conflicts with their fathers.

All this distraction meant I'd forgotten to tape down the lid of the paint can that was sitting on the floor of my parents' car. As I turned the corner I heard a 'pop', followed by the sickening sounds of liquid catastrophe. The back of my parents' car had become a paddling pool. In a panic, I pulled over as thick white paint splashed about my ankles. I tried to scoop it out with my hands. It was pathetic. The scene was the perfect karmic retribution for a serial vandal. Finally, I was forced to surrender all dignity. It was time to call my mum.

She answered with the warm efficiency of a former primary school teacher. 'Hello, Peter.'

'Mum, I've spilt some paint in the car.'

'How much paint?'

'A lot.'

'It's Peter, he's spilt paint in the car!" she called across the house, and in the background I heard my dad's predictably volcanic 'Oh, *what?*' I instantly knew how this would play out. Mum, always in control, would bask in aloof amusement as my dad completely lost his shit. If he got too angry she'd make fun of him. My job was to wait it out.

Driving home, I calculated how to minimise the drama. After twenty-eight years I knew how to emotionally detach from my family dysfunction. I arrived home and made a beeline for the kitchen. Neutral territory. Dad stormed past without a word. He started freaking out when he got to the car, but before long he sped off to the Toyota dealership, leaving Mum and me in the kitchen. She was calm and I was vulnerable. My two brothers were out of the house.

My mum's a classically beautiful woman with sharp features to match her intellect. Her hair, once very dark, is now very white, but no less straight. She looks a bit like a portrait by John Singer Sargent: self-possessed and poised to attack. When the mood takes her she can be deadly, and it was from doing combat with her that I learnt the basics of verbal warfare. My mum grew up on a farm with two equally formidable sisters, and parents who made no secret of wishing they'd had sons. Despite all that, her preferred mode of being is light and silly. I've often wondered whether she resents a lifetime of having to act tough. She was certainly tough on my dad.

I sat down at the table. 'Why's he always like this?' I said.

'I don't know,' she replied, but there was something in her demeanour that suggested she did know. So I waited.

Then she came out with it.

'You know he tried to leave us when you were little, don't you?'

I stared at her. 'No …' I said.

'You would have been two, because it was just after Simon was born. He shacked up with an English girl he met on a diving trip. You can't remember?'

'No,' I said again.

'Well, Julian might remember because he would have been four. But you have to promise not to mention anything.'

'I won't,' I said without thinking.

My dad was a high school art teacher, but his real passion was marine archaeology. He, along with his mates, had discovered and dived on dozens of shipwrecks in South Australia and the Solomon Islands. He was a real adventurer and he loved history. So it was a particular sting to discover that the thing I admired about him the most was also the source of our family dysfunction. But Mum was just getting started.

'He was fooling around on this dive trip and everyone knew what was going on! These people were my friends too.'

I could feel everything inside me flipping upside down. For as long as I could remember I'd resented my mother's dominance. I could never understand why she gave Dad such a hard time and why he never stuck up for himself. I just thought *she's mean and he's gutless*, and that was that. But now I could see that she was still hurt by his betrayal and I suddenly understood why she didn't have any friends. How could she trust anyone after that?

'I asked them, "Who *is* she?" because Dad had moved in with her, leaving me with you three boys! I got her name and contacted her parents back in England and told them, "Your daughter is destroying my family." Well, they set her straight and Dad came home. I mean, she was ten years younger than him!'

I imagined my dad walking back into the house with his tail between his legs and everything suddenly made sense.

I asked Mum whether she'd forgiven him and she said yes, but I knew it wasn't true.

'You can't mention any of this to your brothers,' she said again, and I agreed. At the time it seemed like the obvious course of inaction. There was no way we could talk about it. The only safe topic for passionate discussion in our house was politics. But for a rare moment my mum was speaking openly. I knew it wouldn't last.

'I had an affair too,' she blurted out, apparently eager to unload all her baggage at once.

'What?' I said, dumbly.

Mum nodded. 'It happened years before any of you boys were born.'

'Does Dad know?'

'I don't know,' she said, biting her lip.

I asked her more questions but she was beginning to close up again. Her answers became shorter and shorter. We were standing in silence when we heard the front door open. A moment later Dad was in the kitchen.

'It's going to cost $600,' he said angrily, but I could tell he was calming down. My parents retreated to opposite ends of the house and I caught a bus back to my place. My head was spinning the whole way home and it didn't stop until I told my wife the story. Julie understood and I felt better, but I never spoke to my dad about it and I didn't paint a roller that night.

So why am I telling you about this family mess? Well, it's hardly a coincidence that I spent the next six years of my life digging up and confronting Australia's troubled history in a series of public art projects, while simultaneously avoiding any confrontation with my dad. You might say it was a classic case of Freudian displacement and sublimation, but stock psychological explanations only help in retrospect. At the time I felt as though I were groping in the dark at a redemption-shaped object that kept getting bigger and bigger.

Why redemption? Because part of me believed that I could fix my dad's mistake. If I worked hard enough at something really impressive, maybe Dad and Mum would have nothing to regret. Maybe their mistakes could be erased. But that was only half the chip on my shoulder. The other half was my drive to abandon them. If I worked hard enough at something really impressive, maybe I would reach such an altitude that none of their emotions could touch me. Both halves motivated the same basic imperative: *Work hard. Be impressive.*

At that stage of my career I rejected overtly political art. Propaganda seemed distastefully one-dimensional. I disliked the sanctimony and the instruction. Even parodies of political art seemed lazy and sarcastic. But I was about to learn that politics can't be avoided, and why should it be? Why let taste interfere with my growing need to be impressive?

I couldn't have guessed that I was going to Scotland to become an Australian – and nearly get kicked out of art school.

Becoming Australian

Adelaide is a boring city. That's what everyone says, anyway. Sadly, Julie and I had bought into the lie, so we applied to study at the prestigious Glasgow School of Art. Julie was accepted with a small scholarship for her work in fashion. I was merely accepted. We couldn't have been more excited. We were getting the fuck out of Adelaide!

We'd been to Glasgow on our honeymoon two years previously. It must have been the one weekend of the year that Scotland enjoys decent weather, because we were smitten with the place. Once the second city in the British Empire, Glasgow today is half the size of Adelaide and struggling to reinvent itself. In its heyday it was the shipbuilding centre of the world, with direct sailings from Glasgow to Adelaide. In the mid nineteenth century, one in every ten Adelaidians had been born in Scotland. For some reason there's never been much traffic in the opposite direction. Unless otherwise stated, the rest of this chapter takes place in the rain.

I'd been accepted into the art school on the merits of my uncommissioned (illegal) street art projects, so I expected they wouldn't mind those shenanigans continuing in Glasgow. The school provided me with a small studio where I could prepare my work. The city itself provided plenty of ugly walls that could only be improved by street art. Over the next few months my posters could be seen all over Glasgow. I was in heaven – until the media noticed.

I like being in newspapers. I like reading the fumbling quotes from city councillors who say, 'Obviously the images are of artistic merit, but they were installed illegally so *fumble, fumble*.' I like putting people into a position where they're forced to admit that they value property over expression. That's what graffiti and street art are all about. That's what my art school thesis was all about. Unfortunately my supervisor hadn't read it, because the day I appeared in the Scottish *Herald*, she cracked the shits.

'Peter, you've had your fun but now you need to stop,' she said as we sat in her office.

'But that's what I came here to do,' I said petulantly.

'No, Peter. You're here to complete my course, which you will not be allowed to do if you continue with these … *illegal activities*. We've been very tolerant but enough is enough.'

When you're 10,000 miles from home with 12,000 pounds invested in a degree that's going to add absolutely nothing to your employability, silly threats become ominous. There had been zero complaints about my work. I'd deliberately switched to paste-ups, a paper-based form of street art that's easily removed. Everybody liked them, yet the school seemed serious about kicking me out.

I considered stopping, but at the time the street art was the only thing that made me happy. My other passion of washing dishes for six pounds an hour had given me dermatitis on both arms. I was smoking constantly and feeling depressed. We can all agree that depression is boring, so I did the mature thing and twisted my depression into anger. What added to my agitation was the situation back in Australia.

Ever since arriving in Glasgow I'd become 'the Australian guy'. The label gets imposed upon you. It forces you to think about what it means to be Australian, what you like about your homeland and what you'd like to change. I decided to take ownership of that label. After all, I *was* Australian.

But 2013 was the year of a contentious federal election in Australia. Both major parties were promising to 'stop the boats'. That anti-immigration slogan struck me as particularly absurd coming from a nation of immigrants. So I made this …

… and took the train down to London to stick up a few dozen posters. It felt great to blow off some steam, but I'll never forget a man I met that night. He asked me what my poster meant. He was a black guy. Middle-aged. Thick London accent. I told him the poster was about asylum seekers being prevented from entering Australia.

'That's good,' he said. 'Keep the country pure.'

'What?' I said, confused.

'I think it's good. They need to stop 'em, or else it's chaos.'

'But the poster's about the Aborigines,' I said dumbly.

'Yeah, I get it. But what happened to them was going to happen no matter what. What's happening now is different,' he replied.

I thought about that man on the train back to Glasgow. I knew my poster would amuse the cynical, but the design had little persuasive power. It sneered at the dark irony of Australia's identity but failed to cross the political divide. I tried to think about it practically. Functionally. But my mind went to the obvious place. *Empathy is the key*, I thought with glowing satisfaction. But my revelation would have to wait. It was time to deal with the school.

I went back to the newspaper and told them about the school's threat to kick me out over the very thing they'd embraced me for. Unsurprisingly, the story blew up. I was contacted by a popular Brooklyn-based blog and pretty soon everyone was talking about it. The school didn't like that. They asked me to come in for another meeting.

'Every time someone googles our name, that story is the first thing they'll see!' the head of school said.

'Well, if you're embarrassed, maybe you shouldn't do embarrassing things,' I suggested.

But I was over it. They were petty. I was petty. The whole thing was stupid. I feel obliged to tell you only because at the time I felt like the world was about to cave in. But it didn't. I agreed to stop putting up my posters for the last month of school and they actually gave me a decent mark. Looking back, I regret irritating my teachers, but it's my nature. I seek out and learn from conflict and I learnt a lot from Glasgow. I learnt to humiliate the petty inflexibility of power. I had a new tool, but I still lacked the confidence to find out what it could really do.

The Burden of Empathy

The best moment of my life acctully for my all famely for my sister and brother we were so happy when my bought us baby lamb so cute very friendly when my brought him home me my brother speacilly my sister she were so happy we never can forget that day ever it was beautiful day for us. we all love baby lamb. I still miss that day that was our memorial day.

After a year in Glasgow, Julie and I came home to Tony Abbott's Australia.

We had a plan to save up fast and bounce back to London. We were determined to charge ahead with our glorious careers, but after a few months the strangest thing happened. We discovered that Adelaide wasn't boring anymore! Maybe it had barely changed and we'd just been jerks all along? Who can say? The important thing was we were ready to stay put. After years of flighty excuses we were ready to commit to our work … I needed a new project.

I thought about the man I met in London who wanted to keep the country 'pure'. The word 'empathy' popped back into my head and I had an idea. I went to an art supplies shop and bought twenty books and twenty pens. I contacted a community group called the Hills Circle of Friends and told them I wanted to meet some asylum seekers.

The books and pens were for them. I wrote a note that read: *Please tell me your story with pictures. I will make your pictures into large posters and tell your story to the people of Adelaide.*

I needed to find someone who really loved to draw. On Australia Day 2014, I met Ali. We were in the park at a large event put on by a group called Welcome to Australia, and a friend introduced us. Immediately I knew I'd met someone special. Ali is the kind of person who immediately puts you at ease with his warmth and generosity. He took two books and promised to draw his story. A week later the books returned. They were full.

Ali's father was murdered by the Taliban when he was a boy, so his family migrated from Afghanistan to Pakistan. Ali grew up there as an asylum seeker. Then his brother was murdered. Ali's mother decided Ali must go to Australia. So Ali went across the sea and was placed in detention, where he started to draw.

I collected eight more notebooks from other asylum seekers, all with amazing drawings. Together with Ali's images, the project

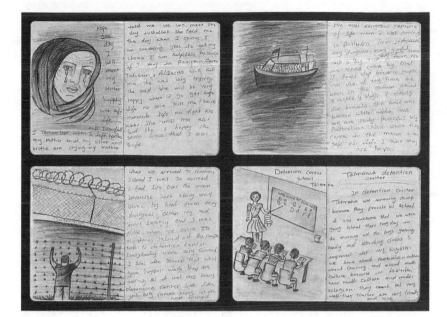

became twenty-four large-scale posters on the streets of Adelaide.

For people who were prepared to stop and take it in, Ali's story was a bottomless reservoir of emotion. You couldn't be human and not feel empathy for him. But Ali's images took time. They couldn't be absorbed at a glance.

I was also beginning to suspect that appeals to empathy carry a deeper problem. Empathy often leaves you feeling vulnerable, and if you're already gripped by fear, the last thing you want is more vulnerability. To those who view asylum seekers as a threat, appeals to empathy can actually be repellent. In this way, the conservative mind is prone to read empathy as weakness. Even liberally minded people can find empathy burdensome. I realised that myself the day I invited Ali to meet my in-laws.

I'd become quite close to Ali. The project had obviously been a boost to his confidence and his sense of belonging in Australia.

I wanted our friendship to continue so I naively attempted to bring him into the fold of my own life. I considered introducing him to my family, but quickly decided against it. Instead I invited Ali to dinner at my wife's family home. It was a special place, the home of four happy children, and now grandchildren. It was a place where anyone would feel safe and welcome.

But despite everyone's best efforts, dinner was uncomfortable. Julie's family were nested within a multi-generational embrace of love and security. They wanted for nothing. By contrast, Ali was alone and had nothing. He hadn't seen his own family in years and his migration status meant he had little hope of visiting his homeland any time soon. It was clear that Ali was aching to be loved but we were divided by an embarrassment of riches.

I came away feeling guilty for having put everyone in that position, especially Ali. Julie insisted that everyone had a wonderful time and I was overthinking it, but I couldn't shake the feeling that it was all wrong.

The immediate effect of empathy is actually pain. Warmth and security only come if we're brave enough to recognise our own vulnerability in the story of another person. Traditionally it's a connection that carries an intimation of the sacred. Perhaps it's something too valuable to be given away through a poster on the street? Perhaps it's something that's fundamentally corrupted the moment it's politicised?

Later that week I saw an elderly woman break down as she looked at one of Ali's images. She was standing there with her husband, and suddenly she lurched forward and started sobbing. I watched as her husband put his arm around her and ushered her away. I felt guilty again. I decided it wasn't the effect I wanted to have on people. I told myself that the decision wasn't personal, but practical. If you had asked me, I would have explained how the images didn't *work*.

I might have said something cold like, 'In the game of image *virality*, the aim is to flatter or empower the viewer, compelling them to share your image with their social network – and they won't do that if they're crying. You want to keep your message fast, shallow and ironic.'

When I think that way, I feel detached and in control. Emotions become like chess pieces. Luckily for me, today's culture rewards the fast and the shallow. If you generate enough noise you can distract yourself from the slow, cumulative effect of detaching from your own emotions. That was my hope, anyway. Because I had plans to make enough noise to escape my own burden of empathy.

In other words, Ali's images were great art, but not great propaganda – and I was beginning to suspect that something in my personality was pulling me towards the propaganda business.

Great Propaganda

So what is great propaganda? How about something like, *Fuck off, we're full!* They're fun words to fart out of your face because of the Fs. Give it a try.

It's fun to pretend, to imagine what it's like to hold the exact opposite of your convictions. It's fun to get as close as you can, to really feel what they feel. You owe it to them, because that's what you're asking them to do for you. That's how I came up with this ...

For anyone unfamiliar with the often forgotten second verse of the Australian national anthem, it goes like this:

> For those who've come across the seas
> We've boundless plains to share;
> With courage let us all combine
> To Advance Australia Fair.

Pretty solid stuff, right? My favourite part is the suggestion of courage. Because why courage? Why not kindness or caring? The suggestion of courage simultaneously admits that fear is inevitable while also providing a solution to fear. You can't cure fear with kindness. But courage, on the other hand, flatters the conservative mind. It's quite different to an appeal to empathy, which can leave the viewer feeling vulnerable and actually *more* susceptible to fear. Obviously the bit about having 'boundless plains to share' is a bit problematic, but we'll get to that.

I invoked the anthem in my launch video for the 'Real Australians Say Welcome' campaign because I think one of art's jobs is to reach back into our history and interrogate the values we claim to protect. I wanted to use the anthem to show that sentiments like 'Fuck off, we're full!' and 'Stop the boats' are actually debasements of Australian values. Removing the burden of empathy and appealing to the very same patriotism that conservatives want to protect, I thought to myself, could be a novel strategy.

At the end of 2014, anyone whose senses were working correctly could detect the storm that was brewing on the Australian political landscape. ISIS beheading videos began appearing in August, and December brought the sixteen-hour Lindt Café siege in Sydney, which shook loose an avalanche of fear. Before we had time to comprehend that the gunman was mentally ill and had no real connection to ISIS, seemingly every Australian had considered the possibility that this was the new normal, that we'd all need to get used to *terrorism* on Australian soil. Then, on 7 January 2015, the Charlie Hebdo shooting erupted in Paris. That sort of fear doesn't just evaporate overnight. It hangs around and searches for answers.

Some people found the answer they needed in the fact that the Lindt Café gunman was Muslim and a refugee. Some of those people joined groups like Reclaim Australia and the United Patriots Front, which quickly attracted media attention despite their meagre membership. Into the limelight leapt Pauline Hanson 2.0. Gone was her anti-Asian rhetoric of the 1990s. The new Pauline was a near carbon copy of her former self, only now she feared 'Islamic terrorism'. Further up the food chain of political influence the rhetoric was less blustery. Those with real power could exploit the growing anti-Islamic sentiment by gradually increasing restrictions against asylum seekers, thereby winning votes.

The feeling was reminiscent of the Cronulla riots ten years earlier, but this time was different. This time all Australians were feeling the fear. Everyone was afraid, but the majority of Australians were able to control their fear and, as a result, resented all the more those who surrendered to their xenophobic impulses.

I don't hate bigots, I hate the bigot in me.

The above phrase popped into my head just now as I am writing this. I think it captures the feeling I've had for a very long time. I know it's not the most popular sentiment, but I really believe that it's the most powerful way to confront bigotry. 'Real Australians Say Welcome' is a way of expressing that idea.

At this point I need to be careful because it's very easy to bestow upon oneself a sense of retrospective self-awareness that exceeds the reality of the moment. In early 2015 I simply had a gut feeling that my poster could capture the mixture of frustration and dismay many Australians were experiencing. Part of me wanted my art to effect 'positive change' on the Australian political landscape, but another part of me wanted something personal. I want to be honest about that part of myself because I think it's something I have in common with many of the people whose views I oppose.

Beneath my carefully crafted image of noble political intentions, I was also hiding a personal desire for self-transformation. At the time I didn't think it had anything to do with my family. It was just a feeling. I wanted to leave my old self behind and this poster seemed like the perfect way to do it. All I needed to do was paddle it out far enough to catch a big wave in the approaching storm. I wanted to play in that storm. I wanted to meet some monsters and do battle. I wanted to see what I was capable of. Above all, I wanted the experience to change me into someone new. Until now my work had attracted the modest attention you might expect for an Adelaide-based street artist. I was a nobody. But I did know a few things about art, especially the power of the *spectacle*.

Street art is a bit like real estate: it's all about *location*. If I'd simply hung my poster in my local gallery, it would have been ignored. If I'd stuck up my posters without announcing my intentions, the response might have been similar. Instead I packaged the whole project into a story, which I could feed to media outlets. I created a spectacle of one artist on a righteous crusade to hold Australia accountable to its own national anthem. In this sense, the artwork is not just the poster design, it's also the journey the audience is invited to follow. By creating a spectacle, my posters could be seen on the street, online and in the news. Multiple locations, multiple exposures, until the person on the street is forced to turn to their friend and ask, annoyed, 'What's with that poster I see *everywhere*?' And with that, you've got them, whether they like it or not.

In March 2015 I launched an online crowdfunding campaign promising to stick up 1000 'Real Australians Say Welcome' posters across the country. The campaign made no mention of asylum seekers. I used footage of the Sydney 2000 Olympic Games in which Julie

Anthony sang the anthem. The tone was warm, inviting and playful. The strategy worked. I raised $8384, more than I needed. It was time to hit the bricks.

Meeting Australia

On 4 April 2015, Reclaim Australia held its first day of nationwide rallies. The next day I checked into the Sydney Central YHA with a roll of 250 'Real Australians Say Welcome' posters in my duffle bag.

The staff at the hostel knew by my hi-vis jacket and workboots that I wasn't there for a holiday, so they put me in one of the dorms filled with labourers, mostly Europeans. It stank, but I knew I was about to make it stink a whole lot more. I went to the nearest supermarket and bought 10 kilos of flour. Back in the hostel kitchen I started to cook my glue, which I poured into the 15-litre bucket I'd brought with me. Someone said, 'That's a lot of porridge! What do you need all that for?' I told them it was glue for my posters. 'Oh,' they replied ... and that was the basic pattern of my youth hostel life for the next three months as I travelled Australia.

I would wake at four a.m. and jump on a train heading in a random direction. Between five a.m. and midday I would stick up thirty posters in good locations as I walked back towards the city. After lunch I'd grab more posters and glue and stick up another twenty in the afternoon. I'd cook more glue in the evening, eat a big meal, then fall asleep early so I could do it all again the next day. It was punishing. After a few days my clothes had built up a layer of organic glue crust. I smelt like blue cheese. I grew blisters on my toes and feet but I didn't care. I was intoxicated by my mission. Nothing could slow me down, except the occasional man on the street.

On the very first morning I met a man in the beachside community of Manly. He was glaring at me as I finished sticking up a poster, his hands in tight fists.

'What do you think you're doing?' he demanded.

'Sticking up posters,' I said in an overly friendly way that was intended to irritate. He looked sixty years old and a few inches shorter than me. Not exactly the monster I'd been hoping to do battle with.

'Oh no, you're not! Not *here*, you're not!' he shouted as he tried to grab my glue trolley.

'Nah, mate!' I said, blocking him with my body. 'That's not happening.'

But he grabbed the scruff of my jacket and growled in my face, 'You're coming with me!'

By now half a dozen people were staring because he was making a lot of noise. In another thirty seconds he'd have help, and then I'd be fucked. Day one of the project, and I'd be in prison. I had to think fast.

'Get off me!' I said with a tone of authority, and broke away from him. In my own head I'd become a man just trying to do his job. But the old guy was persistent. He started to run after me. I ran too, and then I could hear laughter. People up and down the street were watching as the Manly village idiot chased what looked like a council worker with his hi-vis vest and trolley. The man tripped and fell, to the sound of more laughter, and I made my escape. It was pathetic and, as you might have guessed, I felt guilty. Sadly, it became a familiar pattern across Australia.

But I shouldn't overstate the conflict. For every angry old guy, I met a dozen calm ones who weren't too sure about my poster and wanted to chat about it. I'd mention the anthem, they'd say something about 'illegal boat people', and we'd both get on with our day. I was rarely approached by anyone under thirty, and almost never by women.

Picking spots to put up posters is easy. I simply walk through the urban landscape looking for ugliness. If a wall's appearance could only be improved by one of my posters, I make the improvement. That being said, there are a few ground rules. I avoid places of worship and residential homes, although some unit blocks are screaming out for a poster. Government buildings and public infrastructure are up for grabs. I don't think twice about putting up posters on the property of large corporations but I tend to avoid small businesses, unless they have a side wall that's already covered in graffiti. The best spots of all are hoarding boards, abandoned building and underpasses. You'd be surprised how many ugly walls you find once you start looking.

After day four, something unexpected happened: I started to receive messages from asylum seekers who had found me on social media.

This image, featuring the now-actor Ali Morad, was taken in Merrylands, and was sent to me with this message:

Hi Peter. I just thought I'd say thanks … As a teacher of small children who battled the journey here by boat, and my boyfriend, who lost several immediate family members to the Taliban and had every right to seek a peaceful life here … by plane, boat, whatever – that's irrelevant when your life is in immediate danger and there is NO QUEUE to join.

This gave me something real to focus on: the everyday act of welcoming those who needed to hear it. This could sustain me through the daily grind when the major goal of swaying the wider Australian polity seemed hopelessly out of reach. I didn't realise it yet but I was going to need that grounding, because the project was about to be yanked out of my control in the best possible way.

A Meme Is Born

According to evolutionary biologist Richard Dawkins, all forms of human culture can be broken down into units called memes. In his 1976 book *The Selfish Gene*, Dawkins hypothesised that all culture is simply an abstraction of, and reducible to, the biological mechanisms of gene replication. At the time his idea didn't exactly catch fire, but forty years later the idea of the meme found its soaring vindication in the world of online jokes and trolling. I like to think of Mr Dawkins casually perusing these offspring of his intellectual labours. Perhaps he wonders whether the aesthetic quality of Pepe the Frog or Grumpy Cat reflects poorly upon his ultra-rationalist worldview?

I created my first meme back in 2009, while I was going through a stage in which all my work was bike related. After I sprayed the above stencil on a few dozen footpaths in Adelaide, I uploaded the image to Facebook and it quickly found its way onto cycling blogs. People around the world started printing it onto T-shirts, coffee cups, bike helmets and tea towels. At the time it was a thrill to witness the idea take off and find a life of its own. If you google 'this one runs on fat' you'll see that it's still alive and well.

To most people, a meme is simply an image-based joke. However, to a certain subculture of millennials, meme creation and dissemination are almost what rock 'n' roll was to the baby boomers. They hang out on online forums, trading, adapting and evolving memes to shock, amuse and sway their friends. Occasionally a meme floats to the mainstream world of social media, where it attracts a much broader audience. The meme is a powerful concept for thinking about the way culture operates in a post-internet world where every consumer is also a creator, and the entire cultural landscape is democratised into one big toilet wall. In theory, they seem like an attempt to collapse culture into materialism. In practice, though, memes are rarely edifying. Commonly they're malicious. They're all about reduction and debasement.

I've been fascinated with the idea of memes ever since I read Dawkins while I was studying Philosophy back in 2003. And I was thinking about memes the day I designed 'Real Australians Say Welcome'. That's why I made it absurdly plain. The design is almost fascistic in the way the text fills all the available space, leaving no room for any other thought. It's partly that way to ape the xenophobia it aims to parody, but it's also designed to be a successful meme. Without beauty of its own, it can't be reduced. The obvious way it can be successfully adapted into a meme is by adding beauty, which is exactly what happened.

On 12 April 2015 I arrived in Melbourne with 200 'Real Australians Say Welcome' posters and quickly commenced the lonely task of sticking them up. Each day I'd try to convince people on the street to hold the poster for a photo. Sometimes people approached me, which made it easier. The point was to show that people supported the project, that ordinary Australians were literally getting behind the poster to demonstrate their resistance to rising xenophobia. Ultimately, I wanted other people to take ownership of the project. That way its momentum wouldn't be reliant upon my ability to stick up posters. My effort would just be the fuse to light a larger explosion.

On 16 April Julie called my phone after a rough few days of relentless postering.

'Ahhh, have you checked your Instagram recently?' she said.

'Why, what's happening?' I'm usually pretty short with her if I'm in the middle of sticking up posters.

'Have you heard of The Design Files?' she asked.

'No. Should I have? Can you please get to the point!'

Julie explained that The Design Files was the largest design blog in Australia, and they were encouraging their hundreds of thousands of followers to redesign my slogan. They'd issued a callout to 'all the talented Australian artists, illustrators, designers, typographers, stylists, photographers and image makers out there': 'If YOU create a flyer for Facebook or Instagram bearing this message, we'll share it across @thedesignfiles social media, and we'll encourage our followers to share your image too. Any takers?'

'Oh, that's cool,' I said with polite indifference. So Julie slowed down and gave it another try, the way a millennial might explain the internet to a grandparent. She told me that The Design Files is a platform that every young, aspiring creative in Australia dreams of being featured on. While I was approaching people one by one on the street, The Design Files had just incentivised mass creative participation in my project. In 2015, it was what annoying people called a 'game changer'.

'Oh, cool,' I said again, stubbornly. I was probably irritated at the suggestion that Julie knew something I didn't. Understandably, Julie gave up.

'You'll see,' she said. 'Check it again tomorrow and you'll see what I mean.'

So I went to bed and slept the blissful sleep of wilful ignorance, only to receive a call from an ABC journalist the very next morning. The avalanche of attention that followed was pretty staggering. Dozens of artists, designers and illustrators, whom I'd never met, would re-create and embellish the slogan. My original design is crude to the point of comedy. By contrast, their creations were beautiful.

The project had become newsworthy. SBS, *The Guardian*, Buzz-Feed, *Mashable*, *Junkee* and ABC News all ran stories. It was beginning to look less like one artist's crusade and more like a movement. #RealAustraliansSayWelcome was trending across every social media platform. It had taken on a life of its own. It had become a meme.

I promised to be honest, so I should tell you that all that attention was a rush. That kind of attention shakes you up a bit. It's actually frightening, like a new drug. You don't know what it will do to you, so you try not to think about it. You just enjoy the ride as it changes you into someone else. Everything in your mind jumps a gear as obstacles seem to vanish, replaced by opportunities. All the people who know you the best suddenly seem irrelevant, especially your family. Just when I should have called Julie to help calm me down, I didn't. *I've done it on my own*, I told myself. This was exactly what I'd been hoping for. I was inflating into a big, stupid balloon.

Australia the Fascist Construct

One of the first things you'll notice about success is that there's always someone waiting to hate you for it, especially in Australia. I first noticed the contrast while travelling in the United States, where perfect strangers are eager to use you as a springboard for their own optimism.

'You're going to be a great artist,' an American girl once told me. At that exact moment I was more focused on the possibility of becoming a great kisser.

'How can you say that? You barely know me,' I said, a little incredulously.

'I just know,' she said, looking back at me with that self-generated certainty with which great nations manifest their destiny and young Australian men reach out and kiss American girls when they're clearly being invited to. But I couldn't, not back then. I was stuck at that stage when I knew everything but understood nothing. Despite being in my early twenties, I was still nurturing the cynicism of a precocious child. I was all intelligence and no confidence. Who can be confident in a world of infinite possibilities? Obviously she could. She had the warm glow of the believer.

These days I often meet smart kids who are miserable in the way I was for the longest time. That's not to say that I'm perfectly happy now. I just know a kid trapped in a nihilistic funk when I see one. You've got to be careful when talking to them; they're like a person drowning. Sometimes they'll try to pull you down without realising what they're doing. Other times they know exactly what they're doing.

I met some smart kids at the University of Melbourne a few days after 'Real Australians Say Welcome' had blown up in the media. I was exhausted after what had been a hectic week and was keen to put up my last few posters in a safe spot where I could be sure they'd find a receptive audience. I knew the campus had plenty of Morris columns made especially for displaying posters in high-traffic areas, so I spent the afternoon making good use of them.

On the way out I passed Union House, where I'd stuck up a poster on one of the best Morris columns. I gave my poster a self-indulgent glance, only to discover that it had been covered with glossy A3 posters promoting the student elections. I rushed over to investigate. There was plenty of free space on the column, but they'd deliberately gone over my poster. Some student politician was picking a fight with me. Naturally, I took the bait.

I checked the other Morris columns and discovered more of my posters had been covered. The glue was fresh. My rage was hot. Suddenly, there he was. He was using a satchel schoolbag for his posters and a $12 tub of synthetic glue from Bunnings. For some reason he was wearing gardening gloves. Such a hopelessly bourgeois attempt at working-class authenticity made me cringe so hard that it hurt my neck. I just stood there and watched him piss all over my territory with his stupid posters, which he'd probably had printed at Officeworks.

I waited until he'd finished before moving in. I'd seen exactly what he was doing but I still needed to ask.

'What do you think you're doing?' I said with the serenity of a tornado.

'Your poster doesn't belong here,' he said, calmly turning to face me. He didn't even have the decency to act surprised. Instead, he smiled. 'The columns are for Union-affiliated groups only, so you've got no right to be here,' he added.

'This is an art project against xenopho—'

'I know exactly who you are and what you're doing,' he cut in, 'but you should know that your poster is problematic. "Australia" is a fascist construct. We don't need you trying to rehabilitate it. Okay?'

'What about your government-subsidised degree? Is that also a fascist construct?' I asked him.

'I'm so sorry but it's not my job to help you see the big picture.' He gestured at my defaced poster. 'If this upsets you, just remember, this is what dispossession feels like.' He tore off the remaining corner of my poster and walked away in triumph.

I was pretty angry before, but now I lost control. The reptilian part of my brain was calling the shots as I followed him across the crowded campus. He was on his phone and I guessed that he was alerting his comrades up ahead. I didn't care. I was ready to take on all comers.

Across South Lawn I could see our destination, a trestle table covered in posters and attended by three other pasty revolutionaries, already looking in my direction. I charged towards them, my mind racing. I, the slogan master extraordinaire, was about to deliver the perfect ironic witticism to set straight this gang of pubescent agitators. Every student on the University of Melbourne's South Lawn would bear witness. I was going to be proud of this moment.

I marched up to them and shouted '*Fuck your posters!*' at the top of my lungs. Then I flipped over their table and walked away.

An hour later I'd calmed down enough to call my wife. Julie's always ready to laugh at me when I've behaved ridiculously, so I gave her all the details and she lapped it up. Her laughter is the best balm when I'm feeling humiliated. We talked about how much I'd changed since we'd met. I used to be just like the kid who covered my posters. I used to see the world in black and white and hide my insecurities in a foxhole of moral righteousness. It had taken me a long time to learn how to climb out of that hole. I needed lots of help. Julie understood when I occasionally slipped back down.

Still, it's infuriating when you meet your former self and they refuse to listen. You want to shake them until their head pops out of their arse, but it never goes right. I knew that same confrontation was bound to keep happening on this journey. I'd only just begun, and the Australian political landscape is dotted with strange cul-de-sacs where toxic ideas fester. The more attention I attracted, the more confrontation would come with it. But there was a bigger problem: I hadn't really changed as much as I thought. The poster project was dragging me back into my old ways and it would take more than a little table-flipping incident for me to acknowledge it. There was something inherently aggressive about what I was doing, but I thought I had it under control.

I should have been wondering whether all this attention was actually the redemption I was hoping for. I should have been keeping my ego in check. Instead, all I was thinking about was putting up more posters.

The Real Australia

Sydney was done. Melbourne was done. I'd activated the two cities where most of Australia's media was produced. Now journalists could follow the story as I stuck up the remaining 550 posters across the country. For the story to keep growing I knew I'd have to keep generating conflict, suspense, insight, triumph and maybe even redemption and rebirth. To use the argot of our time, I had to keep generating 'content'. How such an empty word as 'content', meaning the literal absence of emptiness, became our default label for the entire spectrum of human drama, I do not know. I'm not content with content. I guess it just sounds smarter than 'stuff'.

The spectacle had really just begun, but now I needed to resupply back in Adelaide. Julie and I were living in a tiny, single-bedroom apartment in Norwood that was physically dominated by our work. We each had a desk at opposite ends of the living space. Julie's fashion label required just as much room as my poster projects, so every available piece of territory was negotiated and fought for. Julie's area was an explosion of vibrant colour, with photos and sketches of Australian flora and fauna covering the walls. She liked to create mood boards for inspiration but they always spilled over the edges. By comparison, my corner was dark, tidy and cold. All I had on the walls were a few sketches of potential poster designs and an old photo of the art critic Robert Hughes. The apartment was our live-in office, but all the hands-on printing happened in my art studio.

Tooth & Nail Studio was the sort of place that scares away people with real jobs. Located in a dilapidated warehouse on Coromandel

Place, in the heart of Adelaide's financial district, it clashed with its surroundings. At first glance it looked unremarkable, just an old brick building next to a pub. Inside it was filthy. It stank of weed, graffiti covered every surface, the roof leaked, the toilet was always blocked and a revolving gang of a dozen misfit artists called it home. Occasionally a curious suit on their lunch break would poke their head past the front door and say, 'What *is* this place?' We'd reply, 'It's a studio, mate. Can I help you?'

Tooth was run by Jake and Cassie, two of that rare breed of creatives who actually have their shit together. Jake dealt with front of house, and Cassie handled the back end. I only saw Cassie when rent was due, but Jake was there all the time. Jake loved to screen-print. It was his shared equipment that allowed the whole studio to function, including my projects. If it weren't for Tooth & Nail, I'd never have gravitated towards screen-printing in the first place.

My little corner was in the basement. With my dad's help I'd customised a rig that allowed me to print the extra-large A0 posters. I'd roll out some kraft paper on an old rug and cut off one sheet at a time, using scissors. It was an absurdly inefficient system. There was no drying rack downstairs, so I used a single wire between two columns to dry my posters. The wire soon filled, so my posters quickly covered every available surface of the basement. I generally printed at night to avoid annoying the other artists.

After a few nights in the studio I was ready to continue. My next target was the Northern Territory, which Hollywood still regards as the real Australia. Most Australians go weeks, months, even years, without contemplating the Australian bush, because most Australians live in cities. When we do confront Australia's centre with any honesty, we encounter a severity that outstrips the sentiments of popular myth. Those endless straight roads are more often a test of endurance than a theatre of romance. But don't let that distract you from the promise of spiritual salvation waiting just over the outback horizon. After all, contemporary Australian art is built upon that myth – upon the world's appetite for believing it and upon our own willingness to dish it up.

It's really the promise of a threshold between the ancient and the modern that makes Australia's centre so enticing. It goes beyond Australian identity towards something universal. It offers an allegory for all people, land, culture and, above all, power. It's our sandy summa of all being and creation. It's unbeatable content.

Imagine all that ancient knowledge wrapped up into an exquisite little canapé. It's being offered to you on a golden tray. It's too beautiful for words. You feel guilty taking it. But what's this? Holding the tray is an equally beautiful Aboriginal child, directed by Baz Luhrmann. The child says, 'It's okay, take it … *Take your experience*™.' That's the Australian tourism industry in a nutshell. That's the Ghan.

I booked a seat on the legendary train. It was a red-class ticket, which is as cheap as it gets. They keep a carriage down the back of the otherwise luxury train for the people who just want to get from A to B. That suited me fine. I was on a very tight budget. Also, I couldn't risk compromising my fair-dinkum, true-blue, she'll-be-right authenticity.

The truth is, I was super excited. This was no ordinary train. I'd first heard of the Ghan on camping trips in the Flinders Ranges. Formerly known as the Afghan Express, the train's name honours Afghan camel drivers who arrived in Australia in the late nineteenth century and played a vital role in exploring the country's interior. Many of the asylum seekers I'd met were from Afghanistan, so I thought this leg of the journey might be a nod to the historic relationship of our two great countries. Originally the name was an insult for the once notoriously unreliable train. Such was the self-assurance that permeated the former British Empire: anything foreign was automatically deemed inferior, and anything local but inferior was automatically deemed foreign.

Our train lurched into motion just past noon. I was sitting next to an older Arrernte woman, who started chatting my ear off. It was one of those distinctly one-way conversations where I'd add a few words every minute or so just to demonstrate that I was listening. But I was listening, because she was a great storyteller. Let's call her Dora.

The sun was setting as we passed the Flinders Ranges and I was having a nostalgic dive into my childhood memories as I stared out the window, but Dora could dive deeper. She started pointing to the shapes in the mountain range that revealed the figure of a sleeping kangaroo. I liked that, so Dora then told me about how she was taken from her mother. That really got my attention. Once she left Alice Springs, she was billeted with families in Adelaide, Melbourne and Hobart. Her stories progressed to her marriage to a man who'd turn his glass upside down on the bar when he was in the mood for fighting; her children, who escaped with her to Adelaide; her grandchildren, who share her warm but fierce temperament; and her great-grandchildren, who show her how to win at Candy Crush.

She spoke for a long time about the importance of Kevin Rudd's historic 'sorry' to the stolen generations, and she also spoke about the importance of forgiveness, but it seemed like a personal forgiveness, too delicate for the words of a politician. She spoke a lot about her granddaughter who drove trucks for the Army. I think she might have been trying to set me up.

I showed her my poster. She looked at it for a while and said, 'Yeah, you're gonna have some trouble with that.'

'What do you mean?' I asked.

'There's plenty of angry people out there who don't want to take responsibility for their place in the world. They want to blame everyone but themselves for their problems,' she said warmly.

'But what do you mean specifically?' I asked.

'Well, there's compassion and there's self-reliance. Sometimes self-reliance is cruel, but so-called compassion can be just as cruel, believe me. One way or another, you're gonna run into trouble with your placard there.'

'That's still not really specific,' I said.

'Neither is your placard,' she said with a 'got you' smile, and I knew she had.

Dora got off at Alice Springs. I got off too. The train was scheduled to stop for a couple of hours as the first class passengers sampled some of the local canapés, so I grabbed my posters and wandered into town. You feel nervous sticking up posters in a small town because everyone knows you're an outsider. Also, this was the Northern Territory. Ever since I'd announced that I was heading north, I'd started receiving messages from concerned followers warning me to be careful. The NT wasn't Melbourne, I was told, and I should watch my step.

I wasn't too concerned. Besides, I had my trusty hi-vis vest to ward off local heroes. I don't know how effective it was but it definitely made me feel a little safer. I managed to get an hour of careful postering done without interruptions before visiting CAAMA Radio for a quick interview. Afterwards I still had half an hour to kill, so a couple of journos from the radio station offered to drive me around town to put up more posters. I threw my gear in the back of their ute and off we went. Now I had an audience who wanted to see some action. It was time to cut loose. We unleashed a postering blitzkrieg on the sleepy town of Alice Springs, hitting spots I normally wouldn't even consider. By the time we pulled into the train yard, the town was vanquished and I was covered in glue. Everyone else had already boarded. I waved to my new-found friends and moments later the train was pulling away.

I repeated the same act in Katherine, just without the help. Considering all the warnings I'd been given, I was a little disappointed to be met with so little resistance on the ground. I wondered why I hadn't been hassled once. It occurred to me that things simply moved a little slower in the north. It's also worth pointing out that it was extremely hot. Within minutes of putting up the first poster I was covered in sweat. That kind of heat makes you think twice about causing a fuss. It also might make you assume that anyone working has a legitimate reason to be doing so. Unfortunately, the other effect that heat has on the human brain is that it makes people go fucking crazy.

Between Alice Springs and Darwin the landscape completes its transition from Australia's central desert to the tropical coastline of the north. Red desert turns to Bullwaddy country filled with millions of monolithic termite mounds and pastoral grasses. As the train rolls north, the scrub gets thicker and greener, then suddenly turns into endless rows of mango trees. They're so plump. The train gradually slows as you pull into Darwin. Stepping out of the air-conditioned bubble, you find yourself in a warm broth filled with insects.

For a city boy from Adelaide, the Northern Territory is like a foreign country. The first thing you notice is that there are Indigenous people everywhere. That makes whiteys like me uncomfortable. We don't like being outnumbered, especially when there's such an obvious divide between white and black. *Why is that Aboriginal man unconscious on the pavement?* you wonder. *It's complicated*, snaps the part of your brain that tries to help you forget about Australia's picture in the attic. But it's not that complicated, really. It's just brutal. I hauled my gear through the sweltering streets. As the sun set, the heat was beginning to penetrate my synapses.

By the time I'd reached my hostel, I was in a foul mood. The dorms were infested with backpackers whose pursuit of 'good times' ran contrary to my righteous crusade. There's nothing worse than a compulsory party. I tried to ignore them and got stuck into my routine of cooking glue before heading to bed. When I woke at four a.m. they were still going. I left quickly. I hit spot after spot as the sun came up, until suddenly I met that guy everyone had warned me about.

Yes, he was another old white guy. I remember being surprised because he was shouting at full volume first thing in the morning. I tried to convince him that the posters were approved by the council, but he was loudly sceptical. Aside from that, though, I can barely remember a thing about him. The truth is, he was boring.

I'd been getting steadily angrier since I got off the train, but running into Mr Shouty sucked all aggro out of me. The confrontation ended with me taking down my poster and moving on, which usually aggravates me even more, but not this time. Instead, I spent the next few days calmly walking the streets of Darwin, at one with the heat, the bugs and the stench of my glue.

I was in this state of equanimity when, on my last day in Darwin, a journalist from ABC's *Lateline* called. They wanted me to fly to Sydney for a profile of the poster project. Suddenly, my Buddha-like tranquillity vanished. The ABC wanted me (and my project) served up on a platter for the whole of Australia! I thought about how to tell the story right, how to put people like Dora and Ali front and centre. I thought about how I could turn the story away from the Mr Shouties. But in all honesty, I mostly thought about me and how much fun it would be to be on TV.

I could still feel my ego inflating. In the next two weeks it would take flight and detach from the semi-sensible parts of my brain. At first it felt great. It felt like the redemptive transformation I had been hoping for. I was floating away from everything, including the old me. But in reality I was about to smash face-first into my father's history.

Courage and Sacrifice

Lateline **didn't need me** for a few days, so I flew back to Adelaide. I arrived on 24 April, the centenary eve of the landing at Gallipoli. Since I was on my voyage to discover Australia, I decided I should attend the dawn service at the war memorial on North Terrace. I found the ceremony to be powerfully moving. It's an eerie experience being among hundreds of strangers, shoulder to shoulder for a minute of total silence. There's no room for detached, ironic participation. You're really there. As the seconds slip away you imagine what it must feel like to hurl your life into the meat grinder of history. Something so terrifying must have its rewards? Or perhaps all the pageantry is just compensation for the barbaric bloodletting? I don't know. Whatever the case, when that bugle finally sounds, you feel alone, and the notes cut right into you.

My brother was in the Navy, but aside from that there's been no history of military service in my family. As boys, though, all three of us were obsessed. It was mostly harmless. We'd compare stats about military ordinances when most kids were swapping football cards. But it started to get weird. I'd wear camouflage fatigues to school on casual days. Kids started calling me 'war boy'. Most disturbing of all, my favourite author was Tom Clancy.

My dad hated it but begrudgingly indulged our obsession, buying us books about warfare and taking us to historic sites. In truth, my dad was just as fascinated by war as we were. He just hated the way us boys had zero comprehension of the horror. When I was twelve, we all visited the Normandy beaches. My brothers and I would slip into fantasy and imagine the thrill of killing the enemy and blowing stuff up. Dad knew exactly what we were up to. He'd always be waiting for his moment to bear down on us with 'it's not fun to have your guts ripped out', or something along those lines.

Despite Dad's best efforts, I brought home from France a very real-looking toy handgun, the kind you couldn't possibly buy in Australia. The only thing that made it look like a toy was a piece of orange plastic inside the gun barrel. I devised a way to remove the offending piece of plastic using Dad's electric drill, but before I could finish the job my gun had disappeared. I asked Dad again and again if he'd taken it but he was a stone wall of denial. I knew he was lying, but what could I do? A few months later I discovered girls and I never read another book by Tom Clancy.

Throughout my life I've seen the Anzac legend grow, through state funding and a culture of mandatory reverence, to become the centrepiece of Australian's national mythology. As a boy I first learnt about Gallipoli through Peter Weir's 1981 film. We watched it in school. Years later I had the experience of watching the film with an American audience in the States, which somehow amplified its effect. It's an odd film, for an odd mythology. Watching it as an adult, you notice that the Turks are hardly in it. The real enemies are the British. The real enemy is imperialism. That's even the way it was taught to us in school.

The film captures something I love about Australian identity: its untheorised dynamism. I'm impressed by the fact that an artist like Weir can make such a powerful statement on Australianness that it rivals any political speech or stately document. But every year the Anzac legend trades a piece of that dynamism for its increasingly monolithic status. There's something cowardly about its dominance.

There's something stingy about the way it's used to monopolise Australianness.

I have a theory that Australia's radical left and conservative right are unwittingly united by a deep lack of faith in Australia. Both sides lack the courage to imagine a bigger, stronger Australian identity. Why not three pillars of Australian identity that offer equal reverence to Anzacs, immigrants (including settlers) and First Australians, united by the notions of courage and sacrifice? That was the point of this poster.

I only printed a handful to see if it worked. Posters need to be simple and I had some worries that this one was too complex. I had a few interesting chats while putting them up on the streets.

'That not right,' one bloke said as I finished off a poster on the back of the Exeter Hotel on Rundle Street. 'Would you parade one of those at an Anzac Day service? It's disrespectful to the fallen.'

I don't like being highroaded, so I let him have it.

'I think comparisons like this can strengthen the relevance of the Anzacs. Imagine if we had a similar level of reverence towards the First Australians as we do towards the Anzacs – it wouldn't hurt. I'm not denigrating the Anzac legend. I'm just saying that it's a good model for improvements to Australia's identity. This centenary could be the high-water mark for the Anzac legend if we don't figure out ways for courage and sacrifice to have a role in our daily lives.'

But he barely looked at me. He just stared at the poster and said, 'Nah, it's not right,' then shook his head and walked away. I didn't blame him. My poster didn't exactly explain *how* we might use courage and sacrifice in our daily lives. I started to wonder whether my poster was a little too ambitious. If it didn't work even after I stood next to it and explained it, it was safe to say I'd bitten off more than I could chew. But my favourite reaction came the following week, from an American.

I'd flown to Sydney for the ABC *Lateline* interview with a couple of spare days to stick up posters. I was putting up the 'Courage and Sacrifice' poster in Kings Cross when I heard an American accent behind me: 'Excuse me, would you explain to me what this is all about?'

I felt immediately at ease. Americans are so polite, and this guy clearly had no skin in the game. I walked him through the poster.

'Oh, I've seen *Gallipoli*,' he said. 'Why do you Aussies celebrate that? I mean, you *lost*!'

For a moment I thought he was joking. But he was genuinely confused. 'There must have been battles Aussies have won,' he went on, 'but you celebrate the one you lost!'

He honestly couldn't wrap his American brain around the idea that sacrifice was more meaningful to our national mythology than notions of victory. I don't blame him; after all, Americans love to win. But most of them love Jesus too, and the Anzac legend is nothing if not a secular adaptation of Christ's blood sacrifice. It's even there in the final freeze frame of Weir's film. Archy dies in agony, arms outstretched, head facing up towards the heavens, crucified.

Maybe my poster wasn't so bad after all? There's always going to be people who just don't get it, so maybe I should judge it by its success rate and not just its rate of error? In any case, I had to focus on the mission at hand. The ABC wanted to speak to me about my current project so I put 'Courage and Sacrifice' aside for another time. The meta-jumble of Australian identity could wait.

I met Jason Om at the ABC's Ultimo Centre in Sydney. It's an intimidating building that triggers my deep distrust of bureaucracy. They make you wait in the central atrium, where I felt out of place in my work gear. All around me I could hear the building hum as it sucked up, digested and excreted vast amounts of information. I'd just walked into the beast's open mouth and politely sat on its tongue. By the time this building was done with my story, I'd taste young, simple and sweet, perfect for mainstream consumption. If I failed to play that role, I'd be spat out, never to return. I was ready to play along.

Jason followed me around the streets as I stuck up posters. I posed inside Central Station and outside the Town Hall. Finally, we stopped for an interview. It went fine. We spoke about how the project had become a movement and how pleased I was that other creatives were getting involved.

Afterwards, Jason disappeared into the ABC building and I walked back to my hostel. I was beginning to feel dislocated from my own story. Someone else was telling it for me. I felt scared and a little bit sick, so I stuck up more posters until the feeling went away.

My Father's Son

I've noticed over the last few years that I've gradually become a bit twitchy when nobody else is around. I'll be working on something when suddenly a shameful memory will appear in my mind, causing me to twitch, grunt or swear. It probably felt good at first, like a little release valve. But sometimes I can't control it. If I'm stressed, it'll happen right in front of Julie. We'll be driving somewhere and during a lull in the conversation I'll drift into my own thoughts then suddenly wince with a short, sharp '*Ahh!*' Julie reacts with shock and concern, but she knows to leave it. She knows when I'm not ready to talk about something. Lately it's been getting worse, which makes me think that I need to reveal some things that I'm not proud of.

After the *Lateline* interview in Sydney I was back in Adelaide for less than twenty-four hours before leaving again for Western Australia. Normally Julie and I are around each other constantly, but over the course of the project I'd already been apart from her for almost a month. We'd talk over the phone every night. She'd be at home lying in bed while I'd be crouched outside my hostel dorm, alone in the corridor. I was enjoying being immersed in my work but I still needed someone to listen to my worries. It was pretty unbalanced but we were accustomed to carrying each other's weight during creative projects. When it was market season, Julie's work came first and I became her pit crew. In that way we fed off each other's ambition, so I bounced in and out of Adelaide without a care.

Since the project had blown up in the media I'd been contacted by dozens of people who wanted to help out. When I announced that

I was coming to Perth I received a message from a photographer who lived in Fremantle. Her name was Sarah. She offered to drive me around Perth and document my process. I turned down most offers for help because postering is really a one-man job. But Sarah's offer was perfect: she'd be out of the way taking photos and I needed a driver.

I'd already been postering for a few hours when Sarah picked me up. I noticed immediately that she was attractive. Not in an obvious way; she had an interesting beauty, which made it worse. My eye kept going straight to her top lip. It had this little dip in the middle that I'd never seen before. We started chatting and the connection was effortless. It felt like a betrayal from the very beginning, as if a boundary had been crossed the moment I said hi.

All day she took photos of me. A good photographer lets you enjoy the narcissism just enough to be in the moment. Sarah was a good photographer. I wanted to be a good subject so I tried to hit some risky spots by climbing abandoned buildings and leaning off the roof to poster the side walls. We stayed out all day, and in the evening some of her friends joined us. Now I really started to show off. I stuck up one poster on a rail overpass while a train went past overhead. I was terrified but acted as if it was nothing.

The next day Sarah took me out again and we continued to have a blast. It was just her and me. I stuck up posters all day and she dropped me off in Fremantle. As soon as she left I missed her. It wasn't a concept in my head. It was a physical longing. I tried to put it out of my mind by putting up more posters. When I got back to the hostel that night I watched myself on *Lateline*. It's a strange experience seeing yourself on TV. More accurately, it's a strange jolt to your ego seeing yourself on TV. It's fame, plain and simple, and my attention-starved ego ate it up.

When I got back to Adelaide I was still thinking of Sarah. Everything around me felt cold. I started to feel physically weak. Day after day a feeling of pain lingered. I had three days to prepare before leaving for Brisbane, and the whole time I couldn't connect with Julie. She was as busy as always but I felt that a door had closed inside me and I was cut off. Emotionally I was completely untethered. Without anyone to speak to, the stuff in my mind was scrambling to find an exit.

I'd been happily married for five years yet I was seriously considering throwing it all away over a feeling that had bubbled up out of nowhere. It made me angry. I felt I understood the whole thing but my understanding counted for nothing. I wanted to change the way I felt but I couldn't. I knew it was my ego gone mad but I didn't know how to regain control. I knew it was because I'd been spending too long away from home. I barely knew Sarah. I just wanted it to stop. Maybe if I waited it would go away?

I couldn't tell Julie. Why hurt her when my current feelings would probably just pass? So I left Adelaide for Brisbane without saying a thing. For three days I put up posters in a miserable funk. This feeling that had taken hold of me was stronger than anything I'd felt in years. Feelings *mean* things, right? Maybe this was the right step for me? Maybe I could just leave everything behind and live in Perth? I had to find out if Sarah felt anything for me. I sent her a message.

> Hi Sarah, I'm sorry if this comes as a weird surprise but ever
> since we met I can't stop thinking of you. If you could figure
> out a nice way of letting me know that I've got it all wrong
> that would be great.

Hi Peter. It was lovely to meet you during your time here …
but this really does come as a surprise.

Yeah, sorry. I think I've just been spending too much time
away from home … I feel better already just admitting that.

No, I didn't. I felt like a complete piece of shit. I'd basically entrusted my marriage to the whim of another woman, who luckily didn't feel anything for me. I was sick with relief and self-pity, so I cried it out like a child. Miraculously I'd been given a whole dorm to myself so I was free to wallow. After an hour or so I felt empty, so I shook it off and went out to stick up more posters.

I decided to just forget about what had happened. I wouldn't tell Julie. What would be the point? Nothing had even happened, I told myself. As I walked around Brisbane I could feel the whole drama melting away into nothing. But in reality I knew that I'd properly lost control. This was a little more serious than losing my shit on the lawns of Melbourne Uni. This time I'd been ready to flip the table on my entire life.

What made it most disturbing was the fact that I'd spent years telling myself I'd never be like my dad. No matter what, I was committed to Julie, and it wasn't a naive promise – it was a discipline. I guarded my attention strictly. My imagination never had time to play outside of my relationship with Julie, so she never had any reason to feel jealous. But despite my best intentions and clever strategies, all it took was a feature on the ABC to tip my ego over the edge, and I'd lost control.

I was sticking up a poster on Wickham Street in Fortitude Valley when an old thought crossed my mind with new force. What if there's something universal, and fundamentally human, about my weakness?

What if that weakness lies at the core of all wrongdoing? Wouldn't that mean I'm really no better than the worst racist? Maybe we're all filled with ancient destructive impulses, lurking deep within us? What if we all lose control from time to time but some of us get lost in our mistakes?

In that instant I knew I had to find a way to forgive my dad. The thought was a long way from becoming action, but I sensed a switch had just flipped inside me. I stayed with that feeling for as long as I could. My body was on auto-pilot as it walked the Valley, sticking up posters. Inside my head, a new feeling was shining a light on the dusty assumptions of my brain. Unfortunately the dust was pretty thick.

It's an uncomfortable idea that there's very little separating you from the things you oppose. It's the sort of idea that you play with for a while, before eventually running top speed in the opposite direction. So the very next day I went in search of some *real* racists to make myself feel better. I shouldn't have trouble finding some, I thought. After all, this was Queensland.

The Heart of Daftness

Along with the Northern Territory, Queensland was the other place that people couldn't wait to warn me about … Actually, I was also warned about Tasmania. Come to think of it, the only place I definitely *wasn't* warned about was Melbourne. So, allow me to warn you: Melbourne is where all the other cities dump their most annoying wankers. I'd hate Melbourne if it wasn't filled with all my old friends from Adelaide.

In Brisbane I knew nobody. Brisbane was lonely in the best possible way. I needed some alone time. When I'm feeling disgusted with myself I tend to project my contempt outwards, at anyone within throwing distance. Luckily I could sublimate my defective personality into a wholesome activity. I was sticking up posters at a cracking pace. If anything, I needed to slow down, or perhaps find a special target for my last few dozen.

My friends had told me that Queensland was full of racists but, sadly, I'd encountered none. Instead, my social media feed was full of people getting behind my poster with big smiles of support. It didn't sit right with my mood. Where was the conflict? I wanted to go out and find it, get right in its face, stir it up a bit, then exploit it for likes on social media. I decided to set out on a little racist safari, so I gathered up what was left of my posters and set off for Roma Street train station. I was going to visit Pauline Hanson's old stomping ground. I was on a mission to Australia's heart of daftness. I was going to Ipswich.

Imagine my disappointment when I discovered that Ipswich was practically within walking distance of Brisbane. I needed something more adventurous, so I bought a ticket for Toowoomba. It was further away, more rural and therefore more racist. I could visit Ipswich on the way back.

After a beautiful train ride through the lush countryside I arrived in Toowoomba to discover a town in the middle of its own street art festival. The First Coat Intl' Art Festival boasted an impressive, multicultural rollcall of artists and performers that threatened to shatter my fantasy of Toowoomba as a bigoted, rural backwater. But I wasn't fooled. I was determined to find the real Toowoomba. I walked away from the murals, music and happy crowds. I walked to the quieter side of town, where I spotted the Metropole Hotel. From the outside it looked like a perfectly miserable drinking hole. I stepped inside with my posters, expecting to meet the cast of *Wake in Fright*. I was going to show them my posters and get a reaction. Instead I met Mohit, who had just arrived from India. Zoey the publican proudly explained that Toowoomba is Queensland's second biggest centre for the resettlement of asylum seekers. I smiled through my disappointment.

I gave away some posters to my new friends at the Metropole before sticking up more around town. Toowoomba had turned out to be upsettingly lovely, but I still had Ipswich. I found the address of Pauline Hanson's old fish and chip shop, Marsden's Seafood. I could walk in there with my poster, cop some abuse and then boast about it on social media to provoke outrage. Plenty of other activists behave that way, so why shouldn't I?

It was almost an hour's walk from Ipswich Station to Marsden's Seafood, so I had time to think. If I went down this path of manufacturing conflict I'd quickly join the tribe of Twitter activists who constantly bait and shame their detractors. I could harvest the abuse I attracted online and never be lacking inflammatory content. Once the trolls caught wind of the fact that I'd happily publicise their abuse, they'd come from miles around to outdo one another. I could sit back and stir the pot, an expression of concerned discomfort on my face for the cameras. Sure, everyone would know I was a feckless hack, but they wouldn't be able to say so without appearing to oppose my righteous cause. 'Better a hack than a bigot' would be my fallback position.

I stepped into Marsden's Seafood with my posters and glue to discover a short Vietnamese lady behind the counter. I stumbled around for a moment, then nervously bought a fish burger combo.

'Do you own this shop?' I asked her.

'Yes, my husband and me,' she said.

'Do you know who used to own it?'

'Yes! Very famous lady,' she said, lighting up with pride.

I discovered that Mrs Huynh and her husband had arrived in Australia twenty-two years ago, seeking asylum. I told her about my posters and she was more than happy to get behind the poster.

As you might expect, the image went viral and provoked a fresh round of media interest. I knew it would. The image was too perfect to resist. As I left Marsden's Seafood Mrs Huynh seemed excited, if a little doubtful at my suggestion that she too might become a 'famous lady'.

As I walked back to the Ipswich train station I began to realise that I'd probably dodged a bullet. If I allowed myself to get sucked into the game of manufacturing and harvesting outrage, there would be no coming back. I'd be complicit in a toxic cycle. Gradually, my self-interest would push me further towards maintaining outrage rather than resolving conflict. I'd be just another political profiteer. Besides, what could be more condescending than a city boy perpetuating a narrative of rural racism? I had been the daft one, expecting to find racism out in the open. Real racism is usually hidden.

As I returned to my hostel I was reminded of everything that had happened over the last two weeks. It wasn't a neat narrative. It was a swirling mass of hot-blooded nonsense. Alone in my room, I tried to make sense of it all. I wanted to know that there was something in me that was good and strong and impervious to the forces I was playing with, but my doubts were growing.

For the first time since the project started I had a powerful impulse to call home and speak to my parents. I hadn't spoken to them in weeks, which wasn't surprising, but I suddenly wanted to let them know I was okay. I wanted to hear myself tell them, 'Everything's going great.' Maybe that would make me feel better?

However, I had a strong suspicion that my family wasn't at all impressed with what I was doing because it conflicted with their views on immigration. I'd deliberately avoided any discussion of the topic for fear that it would open into a bottomless chasm. I was perfectly happy to confront strangers, but not my own family. Ours was a power hierarchy carefully established over years of polite hostility. Disruption might unleash reservoirs of resentment. It wouldn't even occur to us that we had the ability to heal one another. That was just hippie bullshit.

Being conservative can be a great excuse for avoiding feeling. In my family, the ethic of self-reliance fits perfectly with our emotional estrangement because none of us knows how to express our deep need for one another. We keep it locked up inside until it explodes in weird ways, sometimes with a lot of anger. But I wasn't there yet, so instead I pushed it down and tried to focus on the task at hand. I could always talk to my parents once the project was over.

I was done in Queensland. From Surfers Paradise to the Valley, I'd stuck up a tidy 135 posters. Not bad. My inbox was full of messages of gushing praise and hysterical rage. It was becoming too much to make sense of but, from the outside, the project looked like it was cooking nicely. Media enquiries kept coming in and my social media accounts were growing rapidly. I told myself there'd be time afterwards to figure out what it all meant. For now I just had to focus on the road ahead. Next stop, Tasmania. Then Canberra. I was on the home stretch.

Why I Make Posters

When I got back to Adelaide, Julie noticed straightaway that I was starting to fray at the edges. I was leaving the next morning, so she took me out to our favourite sushi place and we tried to reconnect. It wasn't easy because I was so locked up. I still couldn't tell her everything. The truth is, I haven't even tried to explain it to myself until now. So we ate sushi and the next day I was gone.

It was my first time travelling to Tasmania, and as the plane crossed Bass Strait I could feel my worries disappear behind me. Pretty quickly the snow-scattered landscape below had me feeling like a kid. It didn't look like Australia at all. On 1 June I arrived in Hobart with 120 posters. When I stepped out on the first morning it was painfully cold, and electrifying. I was surprised by Mount Wellington's dominance. Hobart is the only city in Australia where nature seems to loom larger than man. Feeling energised, I got to work. Within two days I'd gone through a hundred posters. Now I had time to take in some contemporary art.

I'd been fascinated by David Walsh since he opened the Museum of Old and New Art back in 2011. It was fun to witness his effect on the Australian contemporary art scene. Here was this math-whiz, millionaire gambler who'd built a world-class contemporary art gallery in the middle of bum-fuck nowhere and given everyone a huge kick up the arse. Suddenly the state-run institutions looked even stuffier. Curatorial staff around Australia could point to MONA and tell their board of directors that it was time to shake things up or get left behind.

I visited MONA with the scepticism of an artist who had gravitated away from contemporary art a long time ago. Much of the reason I make posters comes down to my dislike of galleries. I don't like their assumed authority. I don't like the political games you have to play to please the cultural gatekeepers. But MONA was just the extravagant folly of an atheist millionaire who wanted to use his money to take revenge on the town that had wasted his childhood. That was a folly I could relate to.

As I descended the spiral staircase into the gallery I met some Hobart locals. They were able to attend for free and it was obvious they'd come to have a laugh. I had too. It's a fun gallery. It reminded me of the accessibility of British contemporary art. Now, that attitude is everywhere. Compulsory accessibility. These days people forget that contemporary art once had to be taken seriously.

It's worth remembering that the public art museum is a modern invention. Before the Louvre opened to the public in 1793, the only place most people viewed art was inside a church. A year to the day after King Louis XVI was imprisoned, the French Republic threw open the doors of the Louvre and its citizens rushed in. The first public art museum was born, forever wedded to our concept of the nation state. Just as the Church used art to transmit its values, so too would the nation. But over the next 200 years artists had their own revolution – against the nation, against the museums, against the new establishment. If art was to be a secular religion, it must worship the human imagination, the artist's imagination! That's how we got today's avant-garde, always pushing forward, crossing boundaries, deconstructing, disenchanting and generally running out the clock on the humanist wet dream.

David Walsh gets it. His whole museum is like a thin chuckle into the void. I think of contemporary art galleries as luxury theme parks, only less nourishing because at least theme parks encourage kids to make believe, whereas most contemporary art is designed to strip away our beliefs. Contemporary art galleries are usually just smorgasbords of novelty, a collection of expensive gags – which is fine, but it's not avant-garde. Contemporary art is not leading anything. It's just a luxury subculture like couture fashion or yacht-collecting ... That's one perspective, anyway.

Another perspective is that the art world is a laboratory for political dissent. But it's hard to launch a revolution of any integrity from a position of such glamorous privilege. From the Russian

Constructivists to the Situationist International, art history is littered with the revolutionary aspirations of those who mistook aesthetics for a valid means of dismantling the levers of power. At some point the truly revolutionary artists give up, sell out or, saddest of all, join the communist party. They realise that the art world *is* a laboratory for dissent, but only enough to inoculate the state against any real revolution. The art world is like the kidneys of the state, filtering out the malcontents in a steady stream of warm, sterile piss.

By now you're probably thinking, 'I'm getting pretty sick of this puerile, anti-art rant. Peter's clearly a part of the "art world", so why doesn't he just get off his high horse and say something nice?' and I sympathise. My posters are part of a counter-cultural movement called 'street art' that grew out of the graffiti culture of 1970s New York. Like all counter-culture, street art and graffiti have been thoroughly co-opted into mainstream culture, but what keeps street art interesting is its connection to vandalism. When freedom of expression meets private property you get vandalism. It's an indelible fault line between two of the bedrock values of Western civilisation. It's a form of art that institutions can only pretend to condone because, when push comes to shove, institutions will always protect their capital investments over the will of an artist.

Sorry. I went negative again. Perhaps this isn't the place for a comprehensive explanation of my political worldview. Perhaps that comes later in the book. Instead I will tell you how I stuck up posters outside MONA and how they got pulled down the next day. At the time it reminded me of a confrontation I'd had the previous week. I was finishing off a poster outside the Queensland Art Gallery in Brisbane when a security guard ran up behind me and yelled, 'Right! Stop! You can't do that here!'

'Yes, I can. This is an art project,' I said, because sometimes that line works. But not today.

He pulled out his two-way radio. 'I've got him here. Call it in.'

I decided it was time to leave. I started to take down my poster.

'Don't touch it!' he barked, but I kept going.

'The poster's gone. No offence had been committed and now I want to leave,' I said.

'Stay here. We have you on video attempting to vandalise this precinct. The police are on their way.'

It was obvious he wasn't allowed to restrain me physically, otherwise he wouldn't be trying so hard to intimidate me. So I started to run. He started to chase. My kit is compact enough that I can move pretty fast, but I could hear his boots hitting the pavement right behind me. Suddenly, on the corner of Grey Street, he grabbed me.

'Stop! Now!' He'd taken hold of the duffle bag on my back. It yanked at my shoulders. I yanked back. Pulling with all my weight, I charged into the oncoming traffic. A car slammed on its brakes and the security guard let go. I tumbled onto the asphalt, got up and ran off.

I'm not going to lie – it was heaps of fun. And that's one of the main reasons I stick up posters. At the end of the day I want an adventure with a touch of physical danger, and sticking up posters provides it. Even when you're not being chased there's always a lurking potential for confrontation. I love sneaking about at night, on the lookout for danger. It tunes up your senses and reminds you that you're just an animal.

David Walsh seems obsessed with the idea that we're just animals. Overall his museum reads like an attempt to expose the vanity of human spirituality in favour of free-market nihilism. I enjoyed his cabinet of curiosities but the only value holding it all together is the wealth that acquired it. I left feeling entertained, but that's about it. The next day I caught the Redline bus up to Launceston and stuck up what posters I had left. That night I was invited to dinner at the home of local activists. A group gathered and we spoke about asylum seekers trapped in offshore detention. Hadn't that been the reason I started on this journey? I realised that I needed to get my head back in the game. I'd already wasted enough time pondering the political impotence of the art world. I had a campaign to run.

In a week's time I'd be in Canberra, where I'd try to meet politicians. Over the past ten weeks I'd made as much noise as I could and gathered support from thousands of Australians. Every time I logged on to social media I noticed a new Real Australians Say Welcome meme. The hashtag kept growing in popularity and my inbox was filled with more messages of support than I could possibly answer. I was bringing all that support with me to Canberra and offering it to any politician prepared to take it off my hands. I asked my social media followers which ones I should meet. Some politicians contacted me. I contacted all the rest. A handful responded. This was to be the finale, where all the effort came together to *mean* something. When I started the project I imagined that the finale would feel something like surfing a wave. In reality I felt more like a pine cone trapped in an avalanche.

The Political Ecosystem

I hadn't been to Canberra since 2007. At that time my dad and I had driven across from Adelaide to pick up my brother Julian. He had been working in Canberra for two years when, at the age of twenty-six, he lost his job and retreated to Adelaide. I wasn't surprised that Julian had lost his job. Julian was weird. All three of us boys were weird, but Julian had it the worst. He was the oldest, so he took the brunt of Mum and Dad's struggle to save their marriage. He was our big brother, so Simon and I were meant to look up to him, but we didn't. Anyone who met Julian would notice that he was academically gifted. He's brutally intelligent. At first he used it to defend himself from Mum and Dad's expectations, but he also used his intelligence to separate himself from other people. That's how he got weird. Throughout school he stayed aloof and couldn't handle criticism. As the years slipped by, he never quite managed to join the human race. It was only a matter of time before he got found out as someone who didn't quite fit.

I guess our drive over to Canberra was a rescue mission. I was there to keep Dad company, but we talked even less than usual. Our family wasn't equipped to deal with failure on that level. As the oldest and brightest, Julian had always been expected to achieve great things and, in doing so, provide tacit validation for our family. Now that he'd failed it felt like we'd all failed. Not that we ever spoke about it. We just processed it in private. We met Julian at his apartment, loaded his possessions into the trailer and left early the next morning. The air was thick with tension on the drive home. Between Mildura and

Euston we clipped an emu. It jumped out and hit the edge of our trailer with an explosion of feathers. We didn't have time to react. I watched it disappear behind us. The bird was still standing. It seemed fine, but how could it be? I knew it would find a place to die quietly, out of sight. We got back to Adelaide and Julian moved in with my parents. He's been there ever since.

It had always been my plan to finish off the project in Canberra. I'd decided that this was a political project and it needed a political conclusion. It needed a visible win. However, I also had a personal resentment towards Canberra. I think that part of me wanted revenge for what had happened to Julian and it didn't matter whether it made sense. It was easy for me to access the old anger, and that fuel burns slow and steady. On the flight across from Adelaide I psyched myself up for the final push. I would spend the nights putting up posters and the days collecting photos with politicians. I didn't care who they were. I just wanted names. I wanted to push my poster in Canberra's face until I heard 'Okay, enough! We get it!' Then I might feel satisfied.

I checked into the Canberra City YHA and got to work. Before leaving Adelaide I'd posted a call-out to any Canberra-based videographers who'd be willing to document my visit. I received a handful of credible offers but I chose Oliver because he seemed the keenest of the bunch. I needed someone who wasn't squeamish about the illegalities. If I'd known that Oliver was still in school, I might have picked someone else, but I'm glad I didn't. He showed up, keen as mustard but much more level-headed than I'd expected. Strange, I thought, for an eighteen-year-old. He had a calming effect that seemed to balance out my crazy. We made a good team.

Oliver's sister Rosie drove us around between appointments at Parliament House. I met and took photos with various Greens politicians and a couple of Labor backbenchers, but there were no surprises. In their eyes the poster was obviously an oblique reference to Australia's policy of offshore detention and neither the Liberals nor Labor wanted to weaken their ability to service Australia's xenophobia. The truth is that it's a popular policy. It's an election-winning policy. Everybody knows it's cruel, but it's still popular because it's seen to work.

In the last few years I've often been asked to speak on panels about Australian identity in front of audiences with a strong left-wing bias. Whether it's a community group, church gathering or activist organisation, the pattern is generally the same. The event begins with some throat-clearing exercises, where speakers call attention to the 'loss of empathy' and the troubling 'rise in fear' within the polity. Then, as momentum builds, notions of 'equity' and 'open borders' are thrown about with ahistorical abandon. If spirits rise too quickly, someone will offer the obligatory acknowledgement of Indigenous dispossession as it relates to notions of belonging. 'After all, who really has the *right* to offer welcome?' This creates an opportunity for someone else to say 'intersectional considerations'. Everyone hums in agreement and the discussion spirals deeper into puritanical irrelevance. Hardly any attempt is made to understand the conservative perspective. Even describing it leads to suspicion. Ironically, the real leftists love 'othering', and even dehumanising, the conservatives.

Meanwhile, the conservatives have a different means of self-gratification. At Parliament House I spent a lot of time between appointments hanging out at the Queen's Terrace Café. It made more sense than passing through security eight times a day. There I met a couple of journalists, who gave me a quick tour of the media wing. I also met a man called Keith, who told me he was from the Institute of Public Affairs. Only later did I discover that the IPA was a think tank where people like Keith got together to agree with one another. Keith was small in stature with short white hair, thin-framed glasses and a Canberra paunch. He looked to be in his early sixties but possessed the energy of a younger man. There was a touch of self-parody in his Gordon Gekko–style pinstripe shirt and gold tiepin. He clearly loved being conservative and, without a public profile, saw no harm in showing it off. He had an attitude of amused condescension that suggested he knew who I was, yet he still seemed willing to chat. I invited him to sit and, with little encouragement, he proceeded to politely explain the irrelevance of my project.

'Border security as a political issue is irrelevant now,' he told me. 'The boats have stopped! Offshore detention works as a deterrent and Labor agrees. They have to agree if they want a chance of getting elected. Of course the Greens will squeeze some political capital out of their moral posturing, but that's their game. Even *they* know their insane policies will never see the light of day. That's why it's called posturing. Like your poster. It's just a pose.'

'What about our national anthem? Is that a pose?' I asked, before refreshing his memory of the second verse that boasts of our 'boundless plains to share' for 'those who've come across the seas'.

'Well, that's the difference between a song and a piece of legislation,' he replied. 'I think you know that the anthem's talking about our cosmopolitanism. It's not a blanket invitation to anyone with a boat. Australians are beneficiaries of Western civilisation – we're more than willing to welcome people who share our values.'

'I think you have an impoverished view of Western civilisation,' I told him. 'I also think you have an impoverished view of Australia. We're more than just beneficiaries. We're contributors.'

Keith laughed. 'Well, you might be right about that part, if nothing else.' He got up to leave, still amused as he shook my hand. Then he was gone. Five minutes later I was having a very different chat with Richard Di Natale, leader of the Australian Greens.

The more time I spent in Parliament House, the less secure and permanent it felt. I left with the impression that Australian democracy is a delicate miracle. It seems obvious that humans are a power-hungry species, and democracy works by forcing the most power-hungry among us to share the power we desperately don't want to share. In this sense, Parliament House is a habitat built to manage our will to power, the same way an ecosystem manages a bunch of animals. I had a strong feeling that my natural habitat lay elsewhere.

That night I hit the streets of Canberra for a savage postering sprec to end the project. The one thousandth poster found its home on the front of the Department of Immigration and Border Protection.

I was on such a high that I couldn't stop. Then I got arrested and fined for vandalism. Oliver and I got caught on Northbourne Avenue. I felt really guilty about Oliver. He was just there taking photos, but they still took his details. I remember the younger of the two cops saying angrily, 'I've seen these posters everywhere!'

It was time to go home.

Enough

Dad picked me up from the airport. It was something he was always willing to do. Whenever my brothers or I asked for practical assistance of any kind, my dad would always say yes and put his shoulder to the wheel. He must have a sense of duty in that respect, though I've never asked him. We don't talk to each other about our values. We just show them through our actions.

Julie must have been working, because Dad was waiting alone. He spotted me as I walked up the ramp and he seemed really happy to see me. He knew the project was over. He asked me the standard safety questions: was I arrested, did anyone try to punch me, etc. I gave him the facts and we collected my bags. I was tired.

Even though he's now in his seventies, my dad's still a handsome man. His hair is white and thinning and he has a bit of a paunch but he looks pretty good. The way he moves suggests a life spent in pursuit of physical challenges. He shuffles in a hulky kind of way that conveys a lack of self-consciousness. His mind is always set on the task at hand.

I've inherited most of that. I also have his square features, especially his hands.

As we drove up Sir Donald Bradman Drive, away from the airport, Dad suddenly broke the silence.

'You know Mum and I don't necessarily *agree* with what you're doing, but we're both very proud of you and what you've achieved. You know that, don't you?'

I suddenly felt weightless. 'Thanks, Dad.'

'You've always made us proud with what you do. You work hard and we don't know where it all comes from, but we think it's great.'

'Thanks, Dad,' I said again. On the outside I was just sitting there but on the inside I was floating. It felt so good that I immediately questioned whether I deserved it. I started to feel guilty. I wanted to tell him about everything that had happened, about all my mistakes. I wanted to explain how I slipped up with Julie. I wanted to forgive him. I wanted to tell him about all the people I'd met and everything I'd learnt about Australia. It was a powerful rush, but instead of letting it out, I just held on to it. I couldn't speak. It was too much.

I gave Dad a hug when he dropped me home, then he was gone. I didn't want to sit alone in our little apartment so I went for a walk around Victoria Park and tried to make sense of everything that had happened. I felt like a different person to the one who had designed that poster. Wasn't that what I had wanted in the first place? To be transformed? I couldn't remember.

I sat down under my favourite tree, right in the middle of the racecourse, and wrote in a notebook.

Playing with forces more powerful than yourself will shape you in ways you can't predict …

Pffft! No shit, Socrates, I thought as I read back what I'd written. I thought about all the people I'd met and how they'd often confounded my expectations. Now that I was home I had a strange feeling of sympathy for them all, especially those I'd upset the most. I guess listening to Dad in the car had left me feeling vulnerable, but it seemed there was more to it than that. I was reminded of the notion of universal weakness I'd felt after betraying Julie and, once again, it rang true. I still couldn't grasp how it might apply to my own life but I knew I wanted to find out. I knew that I needed to keep moving forward. I had to push deeper into Australia's identity and my own history. I had a feeling it was going to get harder. I suspected that it was going to twist me in and out of shape, but I had to keep going. There was no point in sitting still.

A bit later Julie came home. It was a Thursday so we went out for sushi. I told her about an idea I was working on for a new poster about Afghan cameleers in Australia. She listened, but it was clear she was running low on patience. I'd been in a self-absorbed bubble for a few months; it was time for me to listen to her for a while. So I did.

Recently I showed Julie those texts to Sarah in Perth. I'd never told her about my moment of weakness, and even though it had been slight and happened three years earlier, it upset her and shook her confidence. Then she opened up about her own moments of weakness. Suddenly it wasn't so bad. As it turned out, neither of us was really that pure. We made an unspoken pact: a loss of innocence for a gain in security.

There's a pattern here. I can't put it into words yet, but I can feel it. Maybe if I explain everything the form will emerge. I need to explain everything about my family and how I grew up. I need to explain everything I've learnt about Australia. You're not going to like it all. I don't like it all myself. But I'm going to stick to my promise to be honest. That's the only way I know to figure it out.

PART TWO

INVISIBLE
BOUNDARIES

The Kamikaze Run Squad

At Glenelg Primary School in 1989 there was a gang called the Kamikaze Run Squad. They terrorised the school for weeks, maybe even a month. The object of the gang was to run out of bounds and yell 'Kamikazeeeeee!' with arms outstretched, like fighter planes. Teachers would shout 'Stop that *now!*' but the Kamikaze wouldn't listen. They just kept running and yelling. That was their secret weapon. That's what made them Kamikaze. I know all about it. I was the leader of the Kamikaze Run Squad. I was six years old.

I got the word Kamikaze from my dad. As I've mentioned, he was a scuba diver. He especially enjoyed diving on wrecks, and his favourite place in the world to dive wrecks was the Solomon Islands, especially Ironbottom Sound off the island of Guadalcanal. Within a radius of about 50 kilometres, you can dive on dozens of American and Japanese ships and aircraft from one of the largest and most decisive naval battles of the Second World War. Our house when I was growing up was scattered with artefacts, books and stories from there. It seemed like underwater adventures were all my dad did before we were born. One photo shows him, underwater in full scuba gear, standing on the wing of a Mitsubishi A6M Zero fighter plane. In his arms is the Zero's 20-millimetre cannon. It's almost as big as he is.

'The Kamikaze would crash their planes into the American ships deliberately,' Dad explained.

'But they'd jump out first?' I asked.

'No, they'd kill themselves as well as everyone on the ship.'

I can clearly remember the feeling of not understanding. I kept asking Dad questions until he started to lose patience. Or maybe he started to regret giving the lesson? Once that innocence is gone you can't get it back and I was the kind of kid who cried when I was stung by a bee – not because it hurt but because the bee died. It seemed pointless and sad. I imagined being a Japanese pilot at the end of the war. They'd tell me to fly my plane but I'd run away and hide.

The gang started out as me, Tim and Dominic. At recess and lunchtime we'd dare each other to run out of bounds. We'd jump the front fence, run around the block and back into the school through the lane on Williams Avenue. We drew up a map and called it the Secret Circuit, or the Circuit for short. Completing the Circuit later became the initiation test of the Kamikaze Run Squad.

One day, Mr Teasdale caught me running the Circuit. He was smoking in the lane when I rounded the corner.

'Stop right there!' he roared through his ZZ Top beard.

I froze, terrified. Mr Teasdale was a scary teacher. He had once shouted so loud that David Oakley pissed his pants in the quadrangle. David now works at Deloitte.

'What's your name?' Mr Teasdale demanded, still holding his cigarette.

I said nothing, sensing my advantage. There was nobody else in sight. It was just him and me, but he didn't know my name!

'What's your name!' he demanded a second time, but now I heard fear behind his anger.

It occurred to me that I should enjoy the moment, so I smiled up at him to let him know I wasn't afraid. I watched his own expression break into rage and he lurched out to grab me. I bolted. As I ran away, the feeling that filled my tiny body was the exact opposite of what David Oakley must have felt the day of his quadrangle humiliation.

I felt far more powerful than a six-year-old boy should feel. After that day I stopped respecting teachers who tried to intimidate me. They just seemed silly. I felt like I'd discovered a secret.

We started recruiting gang members. At first it was just our friends, but later other kids wanted to join. We decided girls could join too, but they had to be tough. Rebecca Clark was the only girl who asked and she was pretty tough, so Rebecca was in. I wrote every gang member's name on the back of the Circuit map and hid it in my book box. Sometimes we had as many as ten Kamikazes running at once. We'd run the Circuit. We'd run the junior primary area. We even started to run the corridor during class. Word spread and soon other kids were doing Kamikaze runs, kids who weren't in the gang, older kids. That's what did us in.

During assembly, Deputy Principal Dowdy declared, 'This running and shouting must stop.' He seemed pretty serious. I decided it was time to cool off for a bit. I took the Circuit map home. Dad found it immediately.

'Peter, what is 'the Kemekasi Run Scwod'? he asked with wide-eyed amusement.

'It's my gang,' I said sheepishly.

'Oh, your gang! And what does your gang do?'

'We just run out of bounds!' I pleaded, but I knew he'd keep pushing.

'You know what Kamikaze means, don't you?'

'Yes, *you* told me,' I said petulantly.

'I don't think you do understand.'

I'd expected him to be angry, but this was different. I knew it wasn't safe for us to be running around on the street, but apparently I'd missed something.

'Kamikaze pilots never came back. It wasn't a game. They died, and their family never got to see them again,' said Dad.

'It's just a name!' I said.

'No, it's not. You need to think about it, and *never* leave the school grounds again! You could get abducted and there would be nothing your mum and I could do. Do you hear me?'

'Yes, Dad.'

I still didn't understand, but I had a feeling that I'd crossed an invisible boundary. I didn't regret it, though. I hadn't hurt anyone and I'd made new friends. The rest of my primary school years would be dedicated to building a resumé of mischievous schemes, mostly harmless. But another part of me went searching for those invisible boundaries. They were hidden in words. They were hidden in pictures. Most of all, they were hidden in history.

Strip-Mining the Archive

When I completed the 'Real Australians Say Welcome' poster project in July 2015, I was keen to build on its momentum. I needed a new project, but it had to be better than the first. It had to avoid rehashing the same message, but I did want to maintain the confrontational but optimistic tone. If I was going to push deeper towards the root cause of xenophobia, I had to explore Australia's history and expose the invisible boundaries that linger within our national identity.

I was propelled by the same naive optimism with which I now write this book. Part of me believes that all social problems have latent solutions that can be solved through a kind of *devout honesty*. If we simply tell the truth, our honesty will manifest miraculous solutions in a way that's so unpredictable it requires a kind of faith. However, the other part of me suspects that we thrive as a species in spite of the truth. That illusions, great and small, are essential to our way of life and can only be replaced by more cunning illusions. That part of me wants nothing more than to humiliate my own naivety by watching how this whole honesty thing plays out. I guess the two halves of my character are united by curiosity. I've drawn a diagram to show you what I mean.

In mid-2015 my curiosity led me towards one of the most infamous episodes in Australia's history of xenophobia, the White Australia policy. When people talk about the White Australia policy they're actually referring to a collection of changing policies over a 100-year period that deliberately excluded non-white people from entering Australia. I'm not surprised by its racism. I'm more surprised by the strange idea that anti-racism should be taken for granted rather than being considered a historic milestone, paid for by the moral striving of a species of primates who are constantly struggling to overcome the exact same impulses that put them at the top of the food chain. Because that's the difficult truth about racism: it actually works as a survival strategy between tribes. Just not within civilisations. Could I condense that notion into a poster? Probably not. I had to start small. I had to do some research. My goal was simple – find some photos of Afghan cameleers who worked in Australia during the White Australia policy. It was an idea that first occurred to me when I was riding on the Ghan.

I created a research account at the National Archives of Australia. I also had some help from a couple of historians at the South Australian Museum. You have to find the reference code for the documents you're interested in. Once you have the code you can request to view the documents. The archivists will pull the documents from the archive and you'll receive an email when they're ready for viewing. You then put aside a few hours to sit in a quiet room at your state library and flick through boxes of manila folders.

During my degree at the Glasgow School of Art, we got rigorous training in academic research practices. We were taught to approach the research objectively, almost scientifically. We were taught to leave our own values at the door and let the research material guide us. We learnt that a good researcher should strip themselves naked until nothing remains but a disembodied eye, floating in space. But I think it's silly when art attempts to be science. After all, empiricism is nihilistic. It's all 'how' and no 'why'. Sure, I approach my research with an open mind, but ultimately I was in that archive to find gold. I'm not a scientist, I'm an educated vandal. My research ethic is simple: get in, get out, just don't get caught.

These are what I was looking for. Under the *Immigration Restriction Act* of 1901, people entering Australia could be issued a dictation test that was actually a covert tool of racial exclusion. If you failed the dictation test, you would be denied entry to Australia. If you passed the test in English, you could be asked to repeat the test in French or German or any other European language until you failed.

During my research I encountered the story of the *SS Clan Ranald*, a Scottish ship that sank in 1909 off the Yorke Peninsula, South Australia. Of its sixty-four crew, only twenty-four survived the wreck. Twenty of those survivors were 'lascar', an old term used to describe Indian or South-East Asian sailors. They were taken to Port Adelaide, where they sat the dictation test. The report from the Australian Customs Service reads as follows:

> Nineteen of the colored crew failed to pass the test although some of the men speak good English. The quartermaster (Lucano Orico) known as No. 18 on examination showed that he not only could read and speak English fluently but could also write the dictation test without any hesitation. Consequently the test must be put in another language than English and one with which he is unacquainted. I would suggest that detective Segerlind be employed for this purpose.

Why the subterfuge? Why bother with a test at all? Why not simply put up a sign saying 'Whites Only'? The dictation test reveals Australia's desire to *conceal* its racism. The test promised to keep Australia white, while providing an adequate veil of deniability to the charge of racism. It serviced Australia's ugliest fears without offending the nation's progressive vanity. Sounds familiar, right?

What complicated matters were all the non-white foreign residents already living in Australia, many of whom were essential to the growing economy. Those residents were encouraged to apply for exemption from the dictation test so they could leave Australia and return unimpeded. The exemption papers included photographs, taken by professional portrait photographers. There are thousands of these images hidden away in the National Archive, just waiting to be discovered. So, thanks to a racist immigration policy, we've inherited a beautiful photographic record of Australia's racial diversity that might have otherwise remained invisible.

There were no good photos of the lascar from the *SS Clan Ranald*, only handprints in black ink. These had an eerie quality of their own. You can see exactly where the sailor pressed his living flesh and marked the page.

The story of the *SS Clan Ranald* is just one example of the many specific histories that tugged at my attention. The stories are so rich that I felt like they could pull my art in any direction. I'd come to the archive to find images of Afghan cameleers, but there were so many great photos. I decided to make high-resolution copies of everything I could find. I would work out how to use the images later.

I spent two long days strip-mining the records at the State Library on North Terrace. I'd collected almost 300 images, but as I looked through them I knew I hadn't quite found what I was looking for. I wanted an image that punched straight through that invisible boundary and clocked you right in the eye. But what 'boundary' exactly? I really wasn't sure.

That weekend, on 18 July, Reclaim Australia held nationwide rallies. I saw them march along North Terrace carrying banners that called for an end to non-white immigration. *How times have changed*, I thought. However, there was also a clear anti-Muslim flavour to the speeches. The more I listened, the more obvious it became that a fear of the Islamic bogeyman was the glue that held their whole movement together. I knew I had to find an image of a Muslim man who chose to live his life in Australia under the White Australia policy, someone who had every opportunity to leave but chose to stay.

On the Monday following the rallies I booked a session at the National Archives in Melbourne. I flew across and, on the second day of searching through manila folders, I found this image.

It would take another six months before I was ready to launch the new project, but the moment I found this photo I knew I had my hero image. He just looked so proud and stoic. Here was a man who worked for a living, who remained defiant towards life's injustices, not embittered by its hardships. Here was a man who would have baulked at our culture of competitive victimhood.

Of course, I don't know any of that for sure. We can only imagine what it was like to be the man in the image. But that's the difference between history and mythology. Mythology is where my curiosity catches fire. After all, I'm an artist, not a historian. Through mythology we can push past the knowable facts of this person's identity as a Muslim man who was born in India but lived and died in Australia. Through mythology he can become more than an identity, he can become a personality. He can embody a story that modern Australians cherish and desire to emulate. The man's name was Monga Khan.

C'mon Aussie C'mon

When I arrived back in Adelaide I noticed on social media that my friend and fellow artist Jake Holmes had designed his own poster that promoted a progressive cause through an optimistic appeal to our national identity.

Jake Holmes with his rainbow-coloured 'C'mon Aussie C'mon' poster design, 2015

I thought Jake's design was brilliant. The phrase 'C'mon Aussie C'mon' evoked 1980s Australiana and encouraged the viewer towards a shared victory. The Irish referendum on marriage equality had passed in May 2015 and now it was our turn. At least, that's the way it seemed from the growing enthusiasm in the media. Opposition Leader Bill Shorten had introduced a marriage equality bill to federal parliament, putting the Coalition government on the spot. Jake's poster presented an opportunity to be part of a movement that might actually yield a tangible and historic change in the law. It was something I wanted to be a part of, partly because my own poster project hadn't been able to gain any such victory.

I contacted Jake and encouraged him to build a project around his poster design. I proposed that we make a video and crowdfunding campaign that promised to hand-print 1000 posters and distribute them around the country. It was based on the model I'd developed for the 'Real Australians Say Welcome' project, but rather than sticking up the posters personally, Jake could simply mail them out. This strategy would pull focus away from Jake himself and allow participants to use the poster and the subsequent hashtag as a platform for their own stories.

One of the things that made Jake's design so strong was the family history that prompted its creation. When Jake was thirteen, his mum came out as gay. As a result, his parents split and his mum moved in with her new partner. Jake's dad married another woman, who already had a son. Then Jake's sister fell in love with her new stepbrother! Obviously, when sexual orientations reveal themselves it can lead to a rollercoaster of emotion, even for the most supportive families. Through it all, Jake emerged as one of the most well-adjusted people I've ever met. His family remains connected and supportive in all the ways that matter. Jake believes that love can conquer all, because he's lived it.

Personally, I hadn't lived it. I was simply impressed by Jake's design and could see that it was perfectly timed to ride the oncoming wave of change. All it needed was to be thrust into the public eye. So we got to work building the campaign and managed to raise $7491, more than enough to cover our costs. The network of supporters I'd developed responded well to Jake's design. We attracted some media attention and started to distribute the posters. Then everything ground to a halt.

On 11 August 2015 Prime Minister Tony Abbott shut down the possibility of a free vote in parliament. Instead, he proposed to take the issue to the next election in the form of a non-binding plebiscite, so every Australian would have an opportunity to vote on the issue. The debate was over for the time being, so Jake and I decided to put the campaign on hold until it could be of better use. The few hundred posters we'd printed remained in a pile at Tooth & Nail. We got on with our lives. Then something unexpected happened. I received a birthday invitation from my younger brother, Simon. It read: *In a month's time I'll be turning 30, so I think it's about time that I came out as gay. You're invited to celebrate the occasion at …*

My initial reaction was to assume my brother was making a tasteless joke. That's how clueless I was. I sent him a quick message to check whether he was being serious. He assured me that he was and I felt immediately delighted – surprised but delighted.

I let Simon know that he could rely on my support. At the time he was interstate for work, and he asked me to help smooth things over with Mum and Dad before he got back. So I caught up with Mum for coffee at the Adelaide Zoo. 'Oh, I've known for years,' she told me. She affected a schoolgirl's glee at being entrusted with Simon's secret for so long. But mostly she seemed relieved. We had one of those rare chats that make you feel more connected, but also lighter.

I planned to see Dad the next day, so Mum promised she'd speak to him that night. I urged her to break the news in a responsible way and resist the temptation to deliberately throw him off balance. She assured me of her mature intentions, but I didn't quite believe her. After all, what's the point of keeping a secret for so many years if you can't enjoy the momentary pleasure of taunting your spouse with its revelation?

Dad was still adjusting when I spoke to him the next day. We spoke at length and it became obvious that he was grieving. In his mind he was saying goodbye to a long-cherished vision of a future in which grandchildren might redeem the past. I wanted to tell him Simon might still have children, but that wasn't really the point. Nor would it have been helpful to lay down a condescending sermon on the toxic effect of the heteronormative assumptions surrounding parenthood. What we both suspected, but neither of us could say, was that Simon might have felt comfortable to come out years earlier if ours was a family in which people were open and honest about their feelings. At the very least, there was a clear contrast between Jake's family and my own. Jake was putting his story into public art projects, whereas my family could hardly speak about the things that matter most. Neither Dad nor I had the courage to confront that guilt, not yet. What mattered was that Simon felt loved and accepted right now. Dad could see that. By the end of our chat he was feeling much better. 'This really doesn't change anything,' he said, and that seemed good enough for now.

I reported back to Simon via email and he was characteristically unresponsive. I guessed he was feeling relieved but really I was only guessing. We hadn't been especially close for several years, following a violent outburst that had put some distance between us. It's a story that's probably worth retelling because I struggle to understand it myself.

Back in 2008, a friend and I hosted a late-night radio show at Radio Adelaide. One night we invited Simon onto the show and all decided to get heroically drunk before going on air. Simon is a little bit shorter than I am but more than a little bit stronger. He's stocky and good-looking like my dad but he also has Dad's short fuse. Unlike Julian and me, Simon likes to dress well, which was the only indication that he might be gay. He has a collection of crude tattoos from his time in the Navy. Unfortunately, one thing he didn't acquire in the Navy was an ability to hold his liquor.

My co-host and I were keeping it together, but Simon was falling off his chair. At one point Simon snapped his mic stand off its perch. I was too drunk to convey my concerns to Simon in a respectful manner. Instead, I said something like, 'Get your shit together, you woeful fucking embarrassment.' Before I realised how insulting my choice of words might be, Simon was climbing across the control desk and punching me in the face.

When I regained consciousness there was blood all over the place. I felt certain that I hadn't hit Simon so it seemed the blood was all mine. The glass door of the studio was smashed. Simon was gone. I raced out onto the street and saw him storming off. I chased him down to attempt a blubbery reconciliation, but the cops intervened and sent me to the hospital, where I cried it out in front of a tired medical student who listened patiently while simultaneously attempting to stitch up my busted lip.

It wasn't much fun, but the weirdest part came when I appealed to Mum to help mend the rift. Simon was living in the family home at the time, so I told Mum in the car one day that I wasn't walking through their front door until he'd apologised. I knew I'd provoked him but I wasn't about to let him off the hook until he'd taken some responsibility for his violence. Mum didn't seem to care. I said it was her responsibility to let him know that violence was unacceptable within the family, but she just scoffed at our 'little tiff'. That set me off. As I lost my temper she started to laugh, which sent me into complete meltdown. She was screaming at me to stop before I realised that I'd kicked my foot through the windshield. She gave me a minute to stop crying before she suggested that I walk home. I staggered off in a daze. I was twenty-five, too old to be having violent temper tantrums. I guess I just snapped. It's one of those memories I wish I could forget. I wish I hadn't lost control. I wish I hadn't put Mum in that position, but I did.

It's difficult to convey or even understand the tensions that pass between brothers. From my experience it's a volatile mix of love, resentment, affection and jealousy. Simon never really apologised, but after a while I just let it go because I intuited that things were harder for him. Besides, he hadn't hit me that hard and I've never been one to hold grudges. I knew he'd apologise when he was ready. I could wait. Sometimes that's all you can do.

On 14 September 2015, Malcolm Turnbull challenged Tony Abbott for the leadership of the Liberal Party and duly became the twenty-ninth prime minister of Australia. As he was a prominent supporter of same-sex marriage, everyone expected him to announce a free vote in parliament. Instead, Turnbull retained the policy to hold a plebiscite after the next election. The following week Simon held his birthday celebrations. He apologised for hitting me seven years earlier and we hugged it out.

Money

Around that time I realised I was about to run out of money. I'd like to avoid writing one of those artist memoirs that seem to float down from a place where money doesn't exist. Instead I want to be open about how I make my money. Unfortunately there's not much to tell.

Before the 'Real Australians Say Welcome' campaign I'd been working in hospitality for ten years, mostly washing dishes. I'd started in 2002; it was my first year at uni and I needed cash while I was studying. Then I decided to be an artist. Had I known that being an artist would mean washing dishes for the next ten years, I might have approached the task with more humility. After all, no chef wants to share their kitchen with someone who's nurturing delusions of a higher station. I thought I could hide my contempt for the job, but the chefs sniffed me out. As a result I was bullied and ostracised, but I deserved it. After a few years of hiding behind my aloof detachment I had to admit that I wasn't entitled to anything better. I belonged in that job, until I'd earned my escape. The moment I flicked that mental switch, washing dishes became bearable. I started to respect the chefs and they respected me. That's how I was able to stick it out for seven more years.

If I'm honest, working in kitchens was better than bearable. It was actually something I needed to help me shake off the baby fat of middle-class adolescence. Besides overcoming my stifling sense of entitlement, kitchens also rid me of my fear of masculinity. Ever since playing team sports as an early teen I had never felt comfortable around groups of guys, at least not the kind of guys that regard themselves as normal. I didn't want to be normal. Under the pressure of intense work, people quickly slip into archetypes. In the kitchen that meant you were either a man or a mum. Boys and girls were placed front of house, where their pretty faces would please the customers. Back in the kitchen the mums held matriarchal authority and the men won man points by confronting the pain and ugliness of work. My favourite example of this was the way male chefs dealt with injuries. They all had scars to prove their dedication to the job. One chef kept a tube of super glue in case he sustained a serious cut. He'd pour the glue into the open wound to stop the bleeding, then continue service and only seek medical attention after his shift. In that environment I quickly learnt the recipe for masculinity: *Make yourself useful and never let your discomfort be a burden to others*. It's hardly a comprehensive value system, but it's also not a bad place to start.

When I finally quit hospitality it was to start the 'Real Australians Say Welcome' project. I'd managed to save enough money to last six months, but I had no financial plan. For some reason I believed that a business model would coalesce around my enthusiasms if I pursued them with enough vigour. To some extent, I was right.

Since then I've made enough money through selling posters that I can afford to travel around and stick them up. However, all my personal funds come from my other career, in which I shoot and edit videos for commercial clients on a freelance basis. That work started soon after I left hospitality. Having the two separate income streams means that I can maintain a divide between my art funds and my personal funds. Sometimes I'm flush with money made through art, in which case I simply expand the art projects until the money's gone. That might even mean commissioning other artists to produce work. Other times it's simply a case of sticking up more posters or giving them away.

I've never really trusted the clichéd wisdom that art and commerce don't mix, so it irritates me to admit that it's a cliché that I conform to. I guess I'm happy to keep going with whatever feels right.

By October 2015, 'whatever feels right' meant being broke. As a result, I spent the remainder of the year focusing on making videos so I could regain some financial stability. If I was going to improve upon 'Real Australians Say Welcome', I would need enough money in the bank to cover my rent for at least a few months. So I took on as much freelance work as I possibly could, and by the end of the year I'd made enough money to start 2016 with a clear focus on my new poster project. All I had to decide was what I wanted my new poster to say.

Zippole

Julie's grandma is Italian. Her name is Rose but everyone calls her Mamma. On Sundays Mamma has the family around for dinner, but at Christmas and Easter Mamma invites the extended family over to feast on *zippole*. It's not essential to this story, but you should probably know that zippole are anchovies wrapped in pizza dough and deep fried. Obviously, they're delicious. I can usually eat four zippole before I'm full. Then I like to sit back and enjoy the warm chaos of Mamma's house. It's not really chaos – it's more of a dance between the generations, where, over time, everyone finds their own way to balance their personality within the tribe. But it is raucous. Everyone talks at once, so I like to listen.

At Christmas in 2015, my own family were invited for zippole, which meant I could forget about relaxing and having fun. It would have been fine if only Mum and Dad had come, but Julian had also decided to attend. I knew he'd latch on to me and steer the conversation towards one of his pet interests. Ever since Julian had lost his job in Canberra, nobody asked him about his personal ambitions. Simple questions like 'So, Julian, what have you been up to?' became impossible. For the past eight years he'd been up to exactly nothing. He sat at home trolling the internet, which is awash with people like Julian who think of themselves as warriors in a grand political narrative. I didn't want to hear about his petty victories over people he'll never meet. However, it's difficult to have a real conversation with someone when you're constantly trying to avoid stepping on the landmines of their self-loathing. So I tend to indulge his interests. Unfortunately his interests always circle back to the politics of race.

He found me on the back lawn, where I was playing games with the kids. He looks a lot like our mum, only pale. He's fastidiously well groomed, with sharp, handsome features, but his body is soft from lack of use. With manic intensity he accosted me, launching into an anecdote from some dark corner of the internet, oblivious to the atmosphere of jovial harmony. I wasn't sure what meds he was taking but I was sure he was taking too many. Or too few. He was fizzing at the edges like a volcano of words, wrapped in skin. My immediate thought was to attempt to calm him down or tire him out. He was already on to his second anecdote.

'I found the funniest video the other day, it's soooo bad but soooo funny. There's this black guy at the supermarket, and he's going through the contents of his shopping trolley but it's all the worst food with, like, *zero* nutritional value, but he's just soooo happy to be ...'

All of Julian's 'funniest' stories are told for the purpose of laughing at the poverty of black people. Whenever I've confronted him about this pattern he replies that it's 'just interesting', as if his own interests play no part in the matter. Given the slightest encouragement he'll mention Charles Murray's work on the racial differences in IQ scores, as if this controversial research justifies his personal delusions of innate superiority. But I don't hate his bigotry. It doesn't seem right to hate something that's so clearly born of weakness. It's just a wall he's built around himself to fend off his fear that he's fundamentally unlovable. Of course I'm only speculating, but it's based on a strong intuition that my brother and I aren't so different. I stick up posters, he trolls the internet. We might seem like we're on opposite sides of a political divide, but in reality we're both trying to shake off the same feeling of helplessness.

'You know I'm working on a new poster project,' I said, cutting him off mid-sentence. 'It's about a Muslim man who lived in Australia over a hundred years ago.' I guess I felt like throwing some sand in his gears.

'Really. That's *interesting*. Who was he?' replied Julian. His expression had dropped into seriousness and I could see his mind clicking into focus. This actually seemed to be a good way to calm him down.

'His name was Monga Khan but he was no one really, just a man who was born in India and died in Australia. I found his photo in the archives because he'd applied for an exemption to the White Australia policy ... I'm going to stick up his photo all over the country.'

'Why are you going to do that?' Julian asked flatly.

'I want to show that Muslims have been a part of this country for a long time and all the xenophobic hysteria directed at Islam is a debasement of our own identity as Australians.'

Julian drew breath, and then ... 'Well, that's a nice idea but unfortunately it's a naive fantasy. Australia is fundamentally Western, so Muslims can never really integrate without abandoning key parts of their ideology. It's a clash of civilisations. The Islamic civilisation is 1400 years old and it's struggling with the overwhelming force of modernity. They've also been engaged in civil war ever since the death of Muhammad. But the good news is that Islam's problems aren't our responsibility.'

'But the West is not homogenous, it's pluralistic. And so is Islam,' I replied. 'Don't you think there can be positive cross-pollination of ideas? Maybe Islam's traditionalism can counterbalance the West's terminal progressivism, and vice versa?'

'Islam is *not* pluralistic,' he shot back. 'Islam is totalitarian to its core —'

'Well, what are you suggesting?' I cut in. 'You can't ban a religion.'

'But it's not a religion, it's an ideology.'

'Oh great, semantics! So how are you going to control this "ideology"?' I asked, beginning to lose my temper. This was exactly what I feared would happen. I just wanted to play with the kids and have a laugh. Instead we were discussing the fate of Western civilisation under a lemon tree, holding paper plates.

'Well, there are many things you can do, the most obvious of which is to stop Muslims entering the country,' said Julian.

'What, just ban them?' I said.

'Yes,' said Julian, slightly amused.

I shook my head and looked away. I could feel my anger draining out into a cold and heavy sadness. I couldn't look at my brother. I had to stop myself from crying. In that moment I had an intuition that our whole conversation was a substitute for the things we couldn't say. It was all cowardice dressed up as intellect. What we really craved was a personal connection, but instead we argued about politics. I've never been good at reaching out to my older brother. He'd always been the dominant one, the smarter one, the one I looked up to. That admiration had flipped on its head years ago but I hadn't learnt to adjust. What I really wanted to tell him is that he's loved. Because I do love my brother. But the only emotions we've ever exchanged are expressed through conflict. He uses conflict to feel connected, the way healthy people use affection.

'Can we please stop talking about this shit?' I said quietly as I regained my composure.

'Okay,' he said, looking confused.

We separated. I needed a couple of minutes before rejoining the family fun. Little nieces and nephews were rolling around on the grass as the adults chatted, zippole in their hands and smiles on their faces. In this warm bounty, I felt like an emotional pauper. I could argue with Julian anywhere else, but here at Mamma's the contrast was too jarring.

I think it's a lazy misnomer to describe bigotry as a mental illness. It certainly doesn't help to have an overactive sense of paranoia, but the most important ingredient in bigotry is emotional and spiritual poverty. Zippole at Mamma's house is a culinary feast, but it's also a feast of family affection. It can be confronting to newcomers, especially those brought up under the tyranny of Anglo-Saxon table manners. The culture at Mamma's is Italian, but it's also distinctly Aussie. In addition to the pile of zippole there are prawns and pavlova, Malaysian cold rolls and fairy bread. Everyone brings something different and everyone is welcome. I liked that word, 'Aussie'. I decided then and there that 'Aussie' was the only word I needed for Monga Khan.

I didn't have the courage to confront my brother about how I really felt. *Besides, he's not my responsibility*, I told myself. What does spiritual poverty even mean? I didn't know. But I felt there was something in those words, some potential that was struggling to manifest in me, in my family, in Australia. As the year came to a close, I could feel it growing in me like a storm. Actually, I felt more like a battery, fully charged and filled with acid.

The Legend of Monga Khan

Each week at the end of 2015 brought another heart-crushing image from the refugee catastrophe that was unfolding in the Mediterranean. For every image that provoked empathy, many more provoked fear. That year over a million migrants and refugees entered Europe via illegal channels. Most came from Syria and Afghanistan. Every night the world news supplied a televised tsunami of dark-skinned desperation crashing through the borders of Europe. Conservative Australia sighed its concerns, but the prevailing sentiment remained 'thank god *we* have secure borders'.

There was little hope to be found in the here and now, which made me all the more driven to launch a project with some historic scope. The photos I'd found in the archive were an escape hatch from our present reality. They offered a chance to escape my life in Adelaide and embark on another adventure on the streets of Australia. I wanted to forget about my family. I wanted to forget about work and my crummy little apartment in the suburbs. By the time 2016 rolled around I was aching to break out. I wanted to re-enter that bubble of my own creation and stay there for as long as possible.

The year began with three solid weeks of studio time, in which I smashed out hundreds of new posters. I entered a kind of productive bliss. The only limitation was my physical stamina, which I was free to test. Each morning I bounced out of bed knowing exactly what to do. I allowed no time for hesitation. Stress became excitement. Fatigue became contentment. Every fibre of my imagination was pointed in one direction, like a trillion tiny compasses. I was ready to stake everything on the project I was building. It was a great feeling. I was consumed with anticipation.

On 25 January 2016 I launched my second national project, featuring Monga Khan and six other images from the national archive. Once again my goal was to stick up 1000 posters across the country, visiting all the capital cities. I released a punchy campaign video that was quickly picked up by a few media outlets. In the video I posed the question: 'Did Australia inherit its identity from the people who created the White Australia policy, or does "Aussie" have more to do with the people who survived it?'

The aim was clear – reform the meaning of 'Aussie' by making Monga Khan famous.

This time the financial support was more than double that of the previous year. I raised $19,426 in two months, twice as much as I needed. The runaway success of the project meant criticism came quickly. In the first week I was reprimanded for not including enough women in the poster designs. Of the seven posters, only one woman was featured. A handful of people took this as an example of a male artist perpetuating women's invisibility in history. I explained that women made up perhaps three per cent of the images found in the archive, meaning that I'd actually presented three times more women than the historical ratio. Still, the resulting discussion did highlight women's lack of mobility at the time the photos were taken.

Another criticism pointed out that Monga Khan did not actually ride a camel, as I had originally suggested when I first publicised the project online. Monga Khan worked as a hawker, selling general goods door to door. While hawkers in South Australia did use camels, in Victoria where Monga Khan worked, hawkers used a horse and cart.

So I had to make a few corrections and apologies before pressing ahead. Ultimately, the constructive criticism improved the project, as is usually the case. The real challenge would be separating the helpful critiques from the malicious detractors. That would come later.

The immediate problem was deciding what to do with all the excess funds. Not a bad problem to have! I thought back to what made the 'Real Australians Say Welcome' project such a viral success. How could I add an element of participation to the 'Aussie' project? RASW became a meme because it was easy to embellish and adapt, but how could you adapt Monga Khan? The image was difficult to embellish without degrading the exact aesthetic qualities that gave it historic status. Then I remembered how I felt when I first discovered Monga Khan's portrait. It was a sense of wonder. I wanted to imagine what it was like to be that man. I wanted to go beyond the knowable facts and imagine a personality, to create a myth modern Australians could connect with. After all, we have 'Waltzing Matilda' to embody Australians' contempt for authority. Why not create a new folk hero to embody our contempt for the White Australia policy?

So with the excess funds I began to commission artists to create works that 'imagined the life of Monga Khan as an Aussie folk hero'. I started by reaching out to the people closest to me. James Cochran painted a stunning large-scale portrait, and Manal Younus penned and performed a poem in the voice of Monga Khan. It was powerful stuff. Through Manal's performance I grasped art's power to reanimate values lost to the past. Manal gave voice to the resilience of Monga Khan the folk hero in a way that my poster could only hint at. We were creating something that everyday Australians might accept, embrace and maybe even carry forward. I was very excited – but I would need more help.

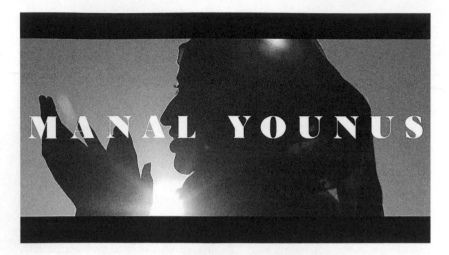

Still from *Monga*, written and performed by Manal Younus

I planned a series of collaborations that I would roll out over the year and that sought to give Monga Khan a life beyond the posters. The ultimate goal was to create a living myth that would take root in the collective Australian imagination. But first I had to get out there and make him famous.

Cronulla and Class

I arrived in Sydney on 1 April 2016 with 250 posters crammed into my brown duffle bag. As I walked into the lobby of the Central YHA I experienced a powerful feeling of déjà vu. *So this is a routine now*, I thought. *This is my routine adventure*. Once again I bought flour from the Woolworths in Haymarket and cooked glue in the hostel kitchen. I was standing by the hot stove, stirring my glue and contemplating the contradiction of my 'routine adventure', when a voice beside me said, 'That's a lot of porridge ... ' At that moment I knew I needed to mix things up.

Since launching the project I'd received dozens of messages from people offering assistance. It was hard to tell who was serious, so I sent out a bunch of replies to test the waters. A message came straight back from Hannah offering a spare bedroom in her family home in Double Bay. I'd actually met Hannah in Adelaide. She was a successful fashion designer and someone I felt I could trust. I looked at the map and it seemed like Double Bay was pretty central. So I checked out of the YHA and jumped on a train.

As I pulled my luggage through the streets of Double Bay towards Hannah's apartment, it occurred to me that I was entering a world where I didn't belong. This was the world of inherited wealth. Palatial homes hid behind perimeter fences on streets lined with cars that cost more than my education. There was zero graffiti, which always makes me nervous. Instead, the landscape was covered with the oddly understated hue of old money. Shining above it all was Malcolm Turnbull's face. His electoral poster smiled down at me from his office on the corner of Edgecliff and New South Head roads. I stopped for a moment and thought to myself, *I'm really going to enjoy postering this area.* I had a week to introduce Monga Khan to all of Sydney but I promised myself to save Double Bay for dessert.

On the following morning I woke before dawn to take the train to Cronulla, arriving just after six a.m. The dawn light was rising over the Pacific Ocean as I passed through Cronulla Park and came to the beach. I was completely alone, with the Art Deco surf club to my right and the rock pools to my left. My immediate thought was, *No wonder they wanted to protect this place.* I'm admittedly a soft touch when it comes to dawn light on a still ocean, but Cronulla beach really is beautiful. Of course, that's not the reason for its reputation.

I savoured the moment. This was to be the location of Monga Khan's debut, but where exactly? I followed the promenade past the rock pools to where North Cronulla beach begins its long impressive arch around Bate Bay. I recognised the surf club from the riot footage.

Back in 2005 the word 'Cronulla' became synonymous with 'race riots'. Tensions exploded after a group of volunteer lifesavers were involved in a fight with beachgoers of 'Middle Eastern' descent. In the hands of radio shock jocks and tabloid media, the fight became an 'attack' perpetrated upon the lifesavers, upon an Australian icon – upon Australia! A text message spread virally across Sydney, calling 'Aussies' to lend their support to 'Leb and wog bashing day' in Cronulla. Thousands of white, angry yobs showed up covered in patriotic paraphernalia. They wrote xenophobic messages on their chests and in the sand. Then they got drunk and started bashing people with brown skin.

Images of white, primal rampage filled the media and shamed Australia. Over the nights that followed, groups of Lebanese yobs carried out retaliation attacks at beaches across Sydney. Then the NSW police came down hard before the violence could escalate. Prime Minister Howard refused to point any fingers and missed yet another opportunity to cut out the rot. Communities have been working to mend the rift ever since.

What's obvious about the Cronulla riots – but rarely said – is that they had as much to do with class as with race. The rioters were losers trying to use patriotism and ethnicity to feel like winners. They weren't protecting the beauty of Cronulla beach; they ruined its name for decades to come. They also vandalised the unifying power of the Southern Cross, and the word 'Aussie'. During the 2000 Sydney Olympics a chant of 'Aussie, Aussie, Aussie' virtually meant 'Welcome to Australia'. After Cronulla, it meant 'Fuck off, we're full'.

I was sick of thinking about it, so I just got to work throwing up posters. I was nervous at first. Then a nice couple on an early morning walk asked me about the poster. I told them about Monga Khan and asked if they'd have their photo taken with the poster. They were happy to. I asked why and they told me, 'Because we're multicultural.' Their names were Lisa and Min.

I left feeling silly for how much time I'd wasted thinking about the riots. For the sake of contrast, I decided to spend the afternoon in Sydney's western suburbs, beginning with Auburn. Every time I unrolled the poster I met a Muslim. It was hard to get any work done. I was going back over territory I'd visited with the RASW posters, but this time there was intense interest. That's how I met Bassam.

Plenty of the people I met knew all about the history of Muslims in Australia, but some of the younger guys had no idea. Obviously I wasn't there to hand out history lessons but it was fun to spark some curiosity and learn some things myself. One man in Lakemba told me about the Makassan fishermen who started visiting the Australian continent decades before European settlement. I'd never heard of them.

In the days that followed I took the Blue Mountains Line out to West Penrith and left a breadcrumb trail of posters across the western suburbs. I liked to think about my images reaching people I'd never meet. Despite the glut of media in today's world, people are essentially information foragers. We've evolved to collect nuggets of information across the landscapes we inhabit. Advertising exploits that impulse, and so does street art, but I think there's something distinct about a message that's placed in a landscape by an individual's own hand.

For the second half of the week I focused on Sydney's North Shore. I visited the SBS building in Artarmon, where Abdullah Alikhil invited me for a radio interview that would later be translated and broadcast internationally in Monga Khan's native language of Pashto.

More help came from a Muslim mother of three who offered to drive me around the Hills District. Mina picked me up in her family wagon with her one-year-old in the back. *This isn't going to work*, I thought, but I was wrong. We covered more ground that day than I thought possible. Whenever I jumped out to hit a spot, Mina came too, pram in one hand, phone in the other. She had that 'get it done' attitude of a mum with a million things on her schedule. By the end of the day I was embarrassed to admit I was exhausted while Mina seemed fine. She introduced me to her family over a delicious Afghan meal. She was an interesting lady.

'I'm a proud member of the Liberal Party because I believe in the empowerment of individuals for the collective good of society, and not the other way round,' she told me, to my surprise.

Mina's ancestors were Arabs who came to Afghanistan to teach Afghans about Islam. They adopted the Afghan (predominantly Zoroastrian) culture while maintaining their religion.

'That's the beauty of Islam,' Mina explained. 'It's dynamic. You can adapt it to any society and any culture. I do whatever I can to highlight that.'

We spoke about Islam's internal struggles to remain pluralist and how federal government grants had been used to recruit Muslim Australians into surf-lifesaving clubs across Sydney, following the Cronulla riots. 'That's how the burkini was invented,' said Mina with great satisfaction. She sent me back to the south side with my stomach full and my head spinning.

On my last night in Sydney I decided it was time to hit Double Bay. I'd had a wonderful stay with Hannah's family. They'd been extremely accommodating of my comings and goings at odd hours and my transformation of their kitchen into a glue factory. So when their eighteen-year-old son asked to come out postering, I thought it would be nice to have some company. Besides, what could go wrong? Well, obviously we got arrested. It was boring and embarrassing, as being arrested usually is, but we did manage to hit some great spots. I was charged with vandalism, to which I would later plead guilty in absentia and pay a fine.

The next morning I said my goodbyes to Hannah's family. It was a little awkward considering I'd got their son arrested, but they were polite enough to downplay their disappointment. I walked back to the Edgecliff train station through the opulence of Double Bay, collecting photos of my posters as I went. Outside the Woolworths I noticed that one of my posters was already starting to peel at the corner, so I decided to make some quick repairs. But just as I jumped atop a bin beneath the poster, I heard a voice behind me.

'Don't you dare!'

I turned to see a woman of about fifty glaring at me through her

Gucci sunglasses. I heard the beep of her camera phone as she thrust it forward. Evidently I was being recorded.

'I'm fixing it,' I said over my shoulder.

'Oh no, you're not,' she said. 'You're leaving it right where it is. This area's *white* enough, thank you very much! The poster stays!'

She enunciated each word with such drawn-out self-congratulation that I was tempted to tear up my own poster just to piss her off. She was, by all appearances, a rich white lady. Her clothes were ostentatiously eclectic. I was still wearing my dirty work gear from the night before. Standing atop a bin, I probably looked more like one of the yobs from the Cronulla riots than her idea of an artist. *How best to dispel her misconceptions in a mature and peaceful manner?* I wondered. Unfortunately, I couldn't think of anything so I just got to work fixing the poster.

'You're being recorded!' she announced.

I finished the job and jumped down. She stood there staring at me through her phone. I couldn't help myself . . .

'Please don't use my poster to racially self-flagellate,' I said, and watched her mouth drop open.

'What did you say to me?' she said.

'It's on your video,' I told her, then walked off towards the station. I wish I'd told her that she should buy some more faux tribal beads if she really hated her own whiteness that much, but the best lines always arrive late.

On reflection, I was surprised that I'd treated her less generously than I had some of the more conventional racists I'd encountered, but at least this time I hadn't flipped over anyone's table. It was irritating being talked down to by someone who clearly had more money than me, but ultimately I was irritated at the failure of the poster itself.

I realised that I couldn't stop people from using my posters to assert the superiority of their class.

On my flight home to Adelaide, I breathed a sigh of relief. Sydney had been a lot to take in. I was leaving behind hundreds of Aussie posters across the city, but I had a growing feeling that something was catching up with me. I still wanted to believe that my posters were bulletproof, but I knew they weren't. There was no way to get involved in this muck without bumping into everyone else's ideas. Wasn't that half the point? Wasn't I meant to be learning? I thought back to Mina, to Lisa and Min on Cronulla beach, to everyone I'd met from Penrith to Lakemba and finally the rich lady in Double Bay. It was too much to process. What had begun as a simple mission to oppose the xenophobes already seemed like a tangled web of invisible boundaries. I decided that there'd be time later to make sense of it all. At the very least, I knew that the Aussie posters were an effective tool for revealing people's true colours.

In the coming weeks I'd stick up hundreds more posters across Melbourne, Perth, Brisbane, Adelaide, Hobart and Canberra. But first I had to go home and get those collaborations rolling.

Cultural Appropriation

Back in Adelaide I made an effort to escape the noise that was growing around the poster project. Just like the previous year, my inbox was full of offers of assistance, media inquiries and rage-filled criticism. I needed space to think. I also needed time to wash down my equipment, deal with the blisters on my feet and print more posters.

For a few days I answered media enquiries and offers of support from random individuals and community groups. Once I had my head above water I contacted the writer Royce Kurmelovs. I had a collaboration to propose.

I'd met Royce years before when he wrote a story about my poster project with Ali. I wanted to commission Royce to edit a book about Monga Khan – a collection of short stories and poems imagining the life of Monga Khan as an Aussie folk hero. We met at a café and I explained to Royce that I had no idea what I was doing. He pretended to believe me and our working relationship developed on that basis.

On the surface the process was simple enough. First, Royce would put a call out for written submissions, then pick the best ones. I'd commission visual artists to produce illustrations. Royce would find a designer to pull it all together. I'd send it to a printer. Everyone would get paid and we'd have a book. Easy! However, beneath the surface of our voyage awaited the sinkhole of political correctness. One wrong move and our project would be sucked down into the vortex. Royce was smart enough to know that it was a real concern. I was smart enough to play dumb.

From the beginning I insisted that we seek as broad a range of submissions as possible. I wanted a cross-section of voices, and I knew that meant risking accusations of cultural appropriation. It's true that Monga Khan was a Muslim and a migrant, but should that restrict non-Muslim non-migrants from imagining his story? I'm neither Muslim nor migrant, yet I'd declared Monga Khan an 'Aussie' and endeavoured to make that claim famous. Surely I'd already decided where I stood.

Of course I had, but I'd never put it into words. So let me be clear right now: I think cultural appropriation is an *anti-cultural* concept that seeks to subordinate culture to politics. By confining creativity within political boundaries, concepts like cultural appropriation inhibit our ability to reimagine and transform group identities. Ultimately, the power of the creative individual is reduced and the power of art to transcend political boundaries is diminished. If you want to make the world less offensive, you need to find a way that doesn't erode the power of art.

I keep circling this point, but notions like 'cultural appropriation' are really just symptoms of a larger spiritual malaise that slides towards nihilism. If you follow it through you'll notice that 'cultural appropriation' presupposes a worldview in which society is just a game of power. That kind of thinking is an impulse we all share, but ultimately it's a reductive way to view the world. Luckily we have the circuit-breakers of imagination, art and culture to keep us safe from ourselves. That said, I don't necessarily fault people who are seduced by ideas like cultural appropriation, especially when they're seeking to protect cultures that have been historically oppressed. I just don't feel comfortable perpetuating the assumption that those cultures are ultimately fragile. To me, that seems a little paternalistic and, ironically, suppressive.

I hoped our little book could pull together a variety of voices and grant the reader permission to imagine Monga Khan as their personal hero, capable of solving their personal crises. Better yet, it might grant the reader permission to identify with Monga Khan, to enter his character via the imagination, thus dissolving the boundary between self and other. To my mind, that seemed a worthy aim, more worthy than obeying the politically correct orthodoxies of the moment.

One day I received an email from Royce explaining that we'd hit a snag. Apparently one of the contributors had pulled out because the book had no Aboriginal contributors. This was actually my fault; from the beginning I'd intended to approach someone I knew personally who was of both Afghan and Aboriginal heritage, but I'd been putting it off out of fear of rejection. But the damage had been done. The vacancy did make room for another Aboriginal contributor, though, so it actually worked out quite well. In the end we brought together eleven short stories and poems and twenty-four illustrations. The back cover reads:

> Monga Khan was born in British India in the area of Batro-
> han in Punjab. He arrived in Australia in 1895 and worked as
> a hawker in rural Victoria. In 1930 he died in the Ararat
> Hospital, aged 68. These are the facts; what follows is
> LEGEND.

There's also a note on the final page of the book stating:

> The Publisher and the Authors acknowledge that the copy-
> right of the fictional character name 'Monga Khan' hereafter
> belongs in the public domain, meaning that anyone can
> publish works of fiction featuring a character of that name.

My original impulse had been to go the opposite way. When Royce and I were working out the initial contracts, I tried to insert a clause that would protect the name Monga Khan as our intellectual property. I struggled with the idea for a week or so before realising how wrong-headed it was. The entire ethos of the project was to launch Monga Khan into collective ownership. I guess I was afraid that if we didn't protect what we created, it might be swept away by a larger entity. Thankfully I realised that the best way to protect Monga Khan was to ensure that he belonged to everyone.

Seven months after my first meeting with Royce, a truck pulled up outside my apartment and delivered 1000 freshly printed copies of the completed book. It would take another year to sell them all, but that first read-through was pure joy. I felt we'd somehow got the balance right. Some of the stories were very dark. Others were filled with whimsy and humour.

Illustration by Andrea Smith for *The Legend of Monga Khan*

Paul Kisselev's illustration of Monga Khan saving Bonnie Hanson from the River Russell as described by Sukhjit Kaur Khalsa in her poem 'Monga Khan & The Humble Hansons'.

Gabriel Cunnett's illustration of Zhen's schoolbag for Elizabeth Flux's short story 'One's Company'.

I'm particularly proud that Elizabeth Flux's short story 'One's Company' was later included in the *Best Australian Stories 2017* anthology, edited by Maxine Beneba Clarke.

Publishing *The Legend of Monga Khan* was a fun experiment in the creation of a folk hero, but I felt that we hadn't risked enough. By all accounts the book was a success, but it wasn't a particularly ambitious project. If I'm honest, the book's greatest weakness was my own lack of expertise as a publisher. If I'd been a little more ambitious and a little less protective, I could have pitched it to a larger company that might have found a wider audience. Instead I did it myself because I thought I could. As a result it became an adjunct to the poster project rather than taking on a life of its own as I'd hoped it might. For all my theorising about cultural appropriation, we actually experienced very little pushback. The conflict was all in my head. We weren't getting in anyone's face. We weren't ruffling feathers. It was fun but it wasn't like putting up posters. That conflict was a real and reliable source of the kick I thought I needed.

Oi! Oi! Oi!

On 12 April I checked into the Melbourne Central YHA with 250 posters ready to go. After my experience in Double Bay I'd realised that I wanted to be alone. I wanted to be away from nice things and nice people. I'd decided that putting up posters is an uncomfortable business and the only way to do it well was by taking pleasure in that discomfort. I wanted to stay in that bubble where my feet ached, my clothes stank and I didn't need to apologise to anyone. I wanted to feel completely disconnected. It's an angry place to be and that anger keeps you going. In the pit of my stomach I had a reservoir of warm acid that was leaking out, one poster at a time.

Days passed with a minimum of human interaction. On social media I would post happy images of people holding my posters, but that was all a performance. On the inside I was obsessed with my imaginary battle against the city. There were five million people out there and it was my mission to reach every one of them – without letting anyone reach me.

Occasionally people would shout at me as they drove by, or try to start a confrontation only to discover that I wasn't the artist they were looking for. I was just a man trying to do his job. Every day I'd wear hi-vis for protection. Practically, it stopped me from getting arrested, but hi-vis also, ironically enough, makes you invisible. It separates you from everyone. You become alone in the crowd, and Melbourne, with all its trams and busy public spaces, is a great city for indulging in that kind of separation. Day by day I drifted further away from people.

By the end of the week I'd almost run out of posters. It was Sunday and Collingwood were playing Melbourne at the MCG, so I decided to put up my last dozen posters around Richmond and catch the football crowd. I had just finished putting up three in a row on Stewart Street when an elderly man snuck up behind me.

'Who are these gents, then?' I heard over my shoulder.

I was caught off guard. He was a small man wearing a red and blue Demons scarf and seemed to be in good spirits. Something about him seemed gentle, so I opened up.

'Well, that's Monga Khan in the middle, Balcoo Balooch on the left and Ackbar Khan on the right. I found their photos in the National Archives.'

I found that I couldn't stop talking. I went on about cameleers, hawkers, mythology and folk heroes, and all the while football fans were walking past the posters on their way to the match.

Finally the man said, 'The shout of "Aussie! Aussie! Aussie!" is so Australian, and combined with those images it really gets to you.'

It took me a moment to realise that the three posters next to each other created the three Aussies of that chant. I honestly hadn't made that connection before, but suddenly it was obvious. Footy fans kept walking past and I'm sure they all made the same connection. There was so much togetherness and warmth in their faces that I had to get away. I packed up my gear and went back to the hostel. I still had a few posters to put up but I couldn't do it. My precious anger had vanished.

The following week I stuck up posters in Adelaide before jumping on the Ghan and heading north. In Alice Springs, Katherine and Darwin I kept putting up posters but I was running on empty. The conflict in me was waning but I didn't want it resolved. Every day I'd receive new messages of encouragement and criticism on social media but I couldn't connect with any of it. More than anything, I felt confused. I didn't know it yet but I needed help.

John

By the time I reached Darwin the wheels were starting to come off the wagon. On the second day I saw a man tearing down three of my posters from across the street and I felt the rage rise up again out of nowhere. Suddenly I was racing towards him. Then I noticed that the police were at the end of the block, and I got control of myself before walking by. The man barely noticed I was there. Back at the hostel I realised it was time to get some perspective on what I was doing. I needed someone to talk to and the only person I knew in Darwin was John, my old uni lecturer. I hadn't seen John in ten years. I don't keep in touch with any other teachers. In fact I barely keep in touch with John, but I knew he'd be good for a chat.

If you're lucky, you'll have at least one great teacher in your life, someone whose enthusiasm for understanding the world is contagious. I was in my early twenties when I found John at Adelaide University. As an impressionable undergrad I'd leave John's lectures with a feeling that the world was somehow larger than I'd been led to believe. Contrary to the spirit of the times, John gave the impression that history was still happening and we were in the middle of it, like voyagers on a vast ocean of hidden currents. The big ideas of history were our vessels and every idea had a lineage and a personality of its own. Best of all, John would listen. If, during a tutorial, you reached out to grab an idea, John would help you catch it from across the room. He'd throw out a multitude of connections and you'd go home wanting to read, read, read!

I met John outside his office in the late afternoon. It would be unfair to say he looked dishevelled, but he didn't look shevelled either. If you imagine a version of Keith Richards who studied Hegel instead of heroin, you will get John's general vibe. He was done for the day so we went to get a drink out on Stokes Hill Wharf. I couldn't tell him what I was going through because I didn't understand it myself. Besides, we weren't close in that way. I just wanted to listen to him ramble and maybe I'd find something I could hang on to.

The wharf was beautiful in a very Australian kind of way. At the end of the concrete pier, overlooking Frances Bay, stood a steel shed with a food court inside. Everything looked cheap and diverse, including the crowd. Darwin is probably Australia's most ethnically diverse city but everyone looks the same in their daggy clothes. There's no point trying to look sharp when the sky's filled with fat tropical clouds and you're sitting in a plastic chair. I ordered a beef massaman curry as John spoke about the legacy of his generation.

'One thing my generation dropped in your lap is the politics of will,' he was saying. 'It's enticing to believe you can fix everything by sheer willpower. John Lennon said, "War is over, if you want it," right? And there's something admirable about that big-heartedness, but it's also very naive.'

'Why?' I said, recognising something of myself in what he was saying.

'Because it's all on the surface,' he replied. 'Underneath the surface, social mores don't change that quickly. The way people put their world together changes very slowly. It comes from the way our mums and dads did it, from our friends. It comes from the way we've learnt to suffer, the way we talk about that suffering and the way we dream of leaping out of suffering. But in the West we've lost our traditions for understanding our shared sense of tragedy. That's perhaps why we've also lost touch with empathy, especially when there's enmity involved, which is when empathy is needed most.'

'But empathy is too painful,' I said, remembering the old woman who burst into tears in front of Ali's poster. 'People talk about empathy as if it's this warm fuzzy feeling, but it actually hurts.'

'That's right!' said John. 'Empathy does hurt, because it's a recognition of shared tragedy. When that recognition is conveyed through art it can be very powerful.'

I thought about this. 'All my poster projects are meant to be about empathy,' I said, 'but I think they're really just an excuse for me to get my anger out.'

'Well, that's the problem with young men!' John laughed without missing a beat. 'Machiavelli made a good point when he said that what to do with young men is a serious political problem.' But John could see that I wasn't joking around.

'What matters is that you're trying to understand yourself,' he said gently. 'Being clever can actually make that process more difficult because clever people are also better at hiding from themselves. But it's important to take that journey because the way we compartmentalise reality can be very dangerous. It blinds us to the way the world is interconnected.'

'That's why it's important to not oversimplify?'

'Exactly,' said John. 'That's why you get these poor kids running off to join ISIS. Many young men go through a nihilistic stage, but usually the culture helps them through it. They learn how to find meaning. But some slip through the cracks. They might shoot up their school or join a religion that promises to make their rage sacred. But for every young man who goes off the deep end there are a thousand more who destroy themselves slowly.'

'I'm pretty sure I'm not that bad,' I said with a smile.

John looked right at me, then said what I needed to hear. 'I think one thing that afflicts young men and women is the disease of absolute certainty. I definitely had a dose of that. Nihilism and idealism are two sides of that coin. But I was a know-all when really I knew next to nothing. When I fell apart emotionally I realised that loving acts are all that matter.'

I was reminded why I liked John. Although I could never keep up with half the things he said, he always managed to leave me with the impression that his own pursuit of understanding was a kind of sacramental rite. He wasn't the sort of thinker who tries to wrangle the universe into his back pocket and call it knowledge. I felt as if John's real aim was to feel humbled and renewed before all that cannot be known. But that meant endless striving, endless pursuit. Something about that appealed to me, but I also doubted whether I had that kind of devotion.

We were joined by John's friend, which took the pressure off me keeping up with John. More food was eaten and drinks drunk before the evening ended at a poetry recital that, as far as I could tell, was chiefly an opportunity for ageing academics to drink and flirt. I made my escape.

When I woke up the next day my head felt calm and clear. The noise had gone. I read the comments on my social media and felt they were from real people. They mattered. This project meant something. I stuck up the rest of the posters, caught my flight back to Adelaide, printed more posters and bounced across to Perth. I was back on the path.

Harjit and Affy holding Monga Khan and Bhagwan Singh.
Two Muslims, two Sikhs, four Aussies.

In Perth I hung out with Harjit and his mate Affy. I'd met Harjit the year before while I was in Perth for the RASW project. I got on with the business of sticking up posters but my mind was still searching. Affy showed me a prayer room in the CBD where Muslims go during their working day. Harjit took me out to the Sikh Gurdwara at Bennett Springs, where I sat in on the ceremony. It was beautiful. When you're in a place like that you can't help but think about the faith of the people present. I'd been thinking about faith since the project began, though I didn't want to admit it.

Harjit runs a program called Turbans and Trust in which he gives non-Sikhs an opportunity to wear a turban. I wasn't going to miss my chance. After I stuck up a couple of posters in the Langar Hall, where worshippers eat after their prayers, Harjit sat me down and started wrapping my head in a bright yellow cloth. It was surprisingly tight. You can see in the photo how it made me feel.

I stuck up 180 posters across Perth. This was the midway point of the project and the media attention was at its peak. The posters had been on the street long enough in Melbourne and Sydney to generate many articles in the mainstream press. All of the attention was positive. That's when you know the criticism is about to arrive – and it did. On my last day in Perth someone tagged me in a photo that shook my little bubble of equanimity.

Cracked

'In reality Australia is nothing but a melting pot of various religious and ethnic groups. While they claim to have a successful multiculturalism programme, there remain entire neighbourhoods in Sydney, Melbourne and other cities which are dominated by one particular racial group, is this success? The reason they will never succeed is because they are trying to unite the population under nationalism, pushing the claim that everyone is Australian ...'

Attributed to Jake Bilardi, January 2015

The copycat posters featured Jake Bilardi, the Melbourne teen who ran away to join ISIS and died in a suicide bombing in Iraq in 2015. He was just eighteen when he died. I'd been fascinated by Jake Bilardi from the moment his story appeared. Obviously he'd been radicalised, but what ingredients lay waiting in the mind of this Australian teenager that allowed him to become easy prey for ISIS recruiters?

Jake was the youngest of six children. Raised closely by his stay-at-home dad, Jake was a sensitive and volatile kid. In his early teens his parents went through a bitter divorce. Under the heading 'I don't feel like this is my home', Jake wrote in his blog: 'Since I was about 11 or 12 years old I have felt sometimes like my home wasn't really my home and that it was all a set-up ... I sometimes even start to question who they [his siblings] are and believe that they're plotting to kill me.'

As a child your confidence in the world is anchored to your parents' love. Our fundamental sense of trust in goodness grows from that point of certainty. We tell ourselves, 'My mum and dad love me and they will never abandon me.' Without that love, we're adrift. Well, Jake's father did leave. And when Jake was just fifteen, his mother died of cancer. With both parents gone, Jake's family home became derelict. His fellow students at school noticed a change in him. He was quieter. He became the target of intense bullying. Then Jake's father reconnected with his son. But the moment they met, Jake was wearing a strange smile. He'd already found a new sense of certainty. Still smiling, Jake delivered his message to his atheist father: 'I've converted to Islam.'

What followed is well documented. Jake prayed peacefully at his local mosque, but was radicalised online. He sought out the ISIS recruiters. There was a flimsy plan to commit atrocities in Melbourne, but Jake's preferred goal was to join his 'brothers' in ISIS. He secured a passport and fell into their loving arms. He appears in ISIS propaganda, joyful to be with his new family and ecstatic at the prospect of dying for their cause. Jake's revenge was complete. He'd replaced his family. His death would prove that his own certainty could replace that which had been torn away from him.

What interests me is this: beneath Jake Bilardi's half-baked ideology, he was just a boy motivated by an ocean of personal resentment, towards a father who abandoned his dying mother, towards a family that fell to pieces, towards the bullies who teased him and a society that let it all happen. What's most unsettling about people like Jake Bilardi is their sanity. We search through the symptoms of their mental illness for signs that they've completely lost their minds so we can draw a clear distinction between them and us. We recoil from the possibility that there is no line. Above all, we underestimate the destructive power of sheer resentment and the need to replace our sense of certainty when the love we relied upon is torn away.

When Jake Bilardi's face first appeared on a copy of my poster there were two possible interpretations. Either someone on the far right was mocking my inclusion of a Muslim (Monga Khan) within Australian identity, or someone on the far left was mocking my aspirational use of 'Aussie'. I really wasn't sure. Then a second poster appeared, featuring the once beloved entertainer turned reviled paedophile Rolf Harris. I breathed a sigh of relief. Clearly this was the work of leftists. I could handle that. Right-wing detractors were dime a dozen. This was far more interesting.

With renewed energy I pushed forward to Brisbane with 180 'Aussie' posters under my arm. I checked into my favourite hostel. Brisbane isn't the greatest city for public transport – if I was going to improve on last year's effort I would need help getting around. Charlotte's offer stood out – she just seemed keener, yet there was something in her phrasing that conveyed a laconic cynicism I knew I could gel with. She arrived in her beloved red 1990 Nissan Pulsar and we proceeded to cut a savage streak across the northern suburbs of Brisbane, putting up posters long into the night.

After a couple of days I was exhausted. Charlotte was keen to keep going but I needed time to catch my breath, so I took the train out to Toowoomba and Ipswich to cover some old territory. It was great to see that some of my old posters had survived and, like the previous year, I encountered more support than criticism.

On the third day, Charlotte drove me around the southern suburbs. I'd just finished putting up a poster when I received a call from a journalist at *The Age*. She wanted to chat about the copycat posters. I lied and said they hadn't bothered me in the slightest.

'Do you know who stuck them up?' she asked.

'I don't know who put them up but I know what type of person put them up,' I said. 'It's obviously someone afflicted by the undergraduate tendency to see all nationalism as something bad. Apparently we need reminding that Rolf Harris was an Aussie and so was the Bilardi kid.'

'Do you think they're missing the point of your posters?' she asked.

'I think they're *deliberately* missing the point,' I said. 'The objective of my posters was to celebrate some Australians who historically had been forgotten and to celebrate the history of diversity in this country.

They're promoting that silly point of view that if something is not 100 per cent good, then you can't enjoy it. They're just being puritanical.'

That was the best I could manage on the spot. The story of the copycat posters was covered by BuzzFeed, news.com.au and *The Independent* in the UK as well as *The Age*. Some of the online discussion that followed was interesting but it didn't go very deep. I let it go and focused on my final day's work in Brisbane. Charlotte was busy that morning so I was on foot in Fortitude Valley. I'd found a great spot on the corner of Wickham and Warner streets and I'd just finished putting up a set of three posters when I heard a voice behind me.

'What kinda Aussie is that?'

I turned to see a man of about sixty-five, wearing a tweed flat-cap. He was almost as tall as me and looked as though he hadn't yet decided whether to be mocking or intimidating. Either way, I wasn't in the mood – so I ignored him and got back to work. He didn't like that.

'He don't look much like an Aussie ta me!' he said, coming close enough that I could feel his breath against my ear.

'You right, mate?' I said. 'I'm just trying to do my job.'

'That's not going to last,' he said, pointing at my poster. 'Not around 'ere, it won't. It won't last five minutes.'

That pissed me off. I'd just spent seven minutes sticking up three posters that I'd printed myself by hand. It was a great spot and I really didn't like the idea that this old coot was going to tear them down as soon as I was gone. If it was just one poster, I might have peeled it off and stuck it up elsewhere, but not three. Besides, why should I cede territory to this guy?

'What's your problem, mate?' I said, turning to face him.

'I don't 'ave a problem, *mate*. You're the one with the problem! You're the one sticking up pictures of terrorists in ma city, and if you don't take it down you're gonna 'ave a bigger problem, meanin' some-one's gonna fix your face for ya!' Now he was really smiling.

'Where are you from?' I asked.

'I'm from 'ere!' he said, gesturing at the ground.

'Nah, you've got an accent,' I said. 'Where were you born?'

'I came 'ere with my pa from Ireland in 1959 and I've lived 'ere my whole life. I'm Aussie! That's not Aussie.' He pointed again at Monga Khan and laughed.

'That man lived, worked and died in Australia. If you're Aussie, then so's he,' I told him, but it just made him angrier.

'We don't need more terrorists in this 'ere place! Now you take it down!'

I glanced around. He was making a lot of noise but there wasn't anyone about who looked like they might intervene. It was just me and the old man, and I'd already decided that I wasn't going to back down. Something in me cracked open. I let it crack open.

'I'll tell you what, I'll take down these posters if you do one thing for me,' I said, wearing a smile of my own.

'What's that?'

I drew in close enough to whisper and look straight into his eyes. 'All you have to do for me is go to your pa's grave and dig those stink-ing green bones out of my Australian soil, you fucking Paddy piece of shit. I want you on your hands and knees, digging that filth out of the ground with your bare hands so you can carry it back to where it belongs, because it doesn't belong here. It'll never belong here, so you just go dig your dead dad out of my country ...'

I just kept going. Once I'd let the anger take control it poured out in an endless stream of bile. I watched his expression break as each word cut into him, but I didn't stop. He started to back away, but

I didn't stop. There were tears in his eyes, but I didn't stop. I let him skulk away.

I was shaking. I picked up my gear and walked off in the opposite direction. As the anger drained from my body, a feeling of disgust rose up from the pit of my stomach. I tried not to look at people as I caught the train back towards my hostel. The feeling kept getting worse. I tried to focus on my breathing but it wasn't helping. As I came down the steps of Roma Street Station, I stepped into the garden bed and vomited behind a palm tree.

When I got back to the hostel Charlotte was calling to help out in the afternoon, so I pushed down my feelings, cooked some more glue and pretended I was still on a righteous mission. We got the work done. I even stuck up my last poster on the front of Pauline Hanson's electoral office. Social media loved it. I felt pathetic.

I told Julie about my confrontation with the old guy, but no one else. I was too ashamed. It's become one of those memories that emerges out of nowhere when you're in the shower.

Recently I was back in Brisbane to stick up posters and I spotted the old guy on the street. It had been two and half years but he was wearing the exact same tweed flat-cap. He was standing there watching people, as old guys sometimes do. I had half a mind to apologise, so I walked up and said, 'Beautiful day,' and gave him a friendly nod.

'Aye, but I'm worried about these trees they've put in,' he said, looking over at a new community garden.

'What's the problem?' I asked.

'Those trees will bring frogs, and frogs bring snakes,' he said, and he was smiling just like before.

I stood and listened to his paranoid wisdom but it quickly became clear that he didn't remember me at all. Maybe our confrontation only lived in my memory? That seemed about right. Maybe I deserved to live with that little piece of unresolved shame. Maybe it's important to remember how easy it is to let resentment take hold. Maybe I'm not so different to Jake Bilardi, or whoever copied my posters. I know how to twist my personal resentments into a weapon and hide it beneath a righteous cause. It's easy to cast the other as an enemy and ignore the personal frailty that motivates their fears. I know how powerful that can make you feel, but I don't like it. I knew I didn't like that kind of empowerment. But I didn't know how to stop.

Canberra

By the time I made it to Canberra, it was the end of August. My inbox was full of messages of support, especially from people of a migrant background, but I'd lost my personal drive. I'd lost that sense of certainty that what I was doing was right. But I had to finish what I'd started.

Unsurprisingly, politicians were far more enthusiastic to have their photo taken with Monga Khan than a slogan like 'Real Australians Say Welcome'. I sent requests to every MP and senator and managed to set up over twenty meetings. This time it was an even split between Labor and the Greens, with a couple of independents thrown in for good measure. Not a single Liberal stepped up, though I did receive a letter of apology from Malcolm Turnbull's office, citing 'existing programme commitments'.

Again, I set up shop in the Queen's Terrace Café. This time I found a nook behind the life-size statue of Queen Elizabeth, cast in bronze by the South Australian artist John Dowie, who'd managed to make the monarch look oddly dynamic. By contrast, I was feeling like a puppet to my own ambition. But there was certainly enough kinetic energy in that building to animate some of the wind-up toys who worked there. Surely I'd fit right in.

Not really. I stood out like an artist in a building full of suits, so it wasn't surprising that Keith found me. I hadn't seen him since we met in the café the year before. I couldn't figure out why he wanted to talk to me until it became obvious that it was for his own amusement.

'I saw your Jihadi Jake posters in the paper. Very cheeky,' he said.

'That wasn't me.'

'Of course, but it's always fun to see the left eat itself,' said Keith.

'Well, you must be equally amused when the right does the same?' I asked. 'Last time we met, the top job still belonged to Tony.'

Keith smiled. 'They won the election, didn't they? But I take your point, the centre's looking a little wobbly these days, but that's exciting! It means there's work to be done.'

'I don't find it fun,' I said.

'Then you're in the wrong place,' said Keith. 'Your problem is that you're a child of the '90s. You've got to realise that the world is unlikely to ever be that peaceful again, at least not in your lifetime.'

I was looking at a man at least ten years my senior, so why did I feel like I was talking to my brother?

'Well, thanks for the tip, Keith,' I said. 'Any other helpful advice?'

'Have you met with Sam Dastyari yet? I'm sure he'd be sympathetic to your cause, although I fear he'll be having a very busy week.'

'We've got a meeting scheduled for Friday,' I said. It was Tuesday.

'Oh, that should cheer you up. Sam's a fun guy.'

Later that night the story broke that Senator Dastyari had asked a Chinese donor with deep connections to the communist government to pay his bill after exceeding taxpayer-funded travel entitlements. The story detailed a disturbing pattern of donations from Chinese interests. Keith was right. Sam did have a busy week. Cory Bernardi and his goons tore Sam down.

For half a second I considered cancelling our meeting. A photo with a disgraced senator was of no use to me, but my curiosity won out. What does a disgraced man look like up close? Besides, who was I to turn up my nose at this guy? Maybe I had more in common with him than I cared to admit.

On Friday it was dark outside by the time an exhausted member of Sam's staff showed me to an empty office.

'Sam will be with you in five minutes. Can I get you anything?' he asked.

I was happy to wait. It had been a long week for me too. I sat alone in the office and stared at the shelves. I noticed they looked strangely bare. On the table in the corner there was a large open box, so I walked over to peek inside. It was filled with Chinese paraphernalia that had obviously been stripped from the shelves. Among the ornaments were photos of Sam standing next to Chinese men in suits. I even recognised a copy of Mao's Little Red Book. *Keith would love this*, I thought, but mostly I thought it was sad.

Sam showed up looking sweaty but still managed to pull his lips back over his teeth in something resembling a smile. I'd expected to meet an older man but apparently we were the same age. We chatted briefly. He'd seen the poster of Monga Khan in Sydney. We had our photo and I left. The following week he resigned from Labor's frontbench. A year later he was forced to resign from the Senate amid further controversy. Apparently Sam didn't know how to stop either.

I am fascinated by people who can't stop themselves from going too far and I feel a certain affinity with that self-destructive drive, but I'm even more fascinated by people like Keith. I couldn't shake the impression that he was just like Julian, only more functional. I thought about him every day until Keith became one of the characters who lived inside my head. I indulged in imaginary confrontations, long arguments where Keith and Julian were one and the same person. My wife noticed that I was twitching again. She'd ask me what was wrong, what I was thinking about. I'd tell her it was nothing and try to chat about something neutral but it was only a matter of time before I'd go back to thinking about Keith.

My poster project had come to an end but I didn't feel resolved. After what had happened in Brisbane, I knew there wasn't going to be a happy ending. From the outside everything looked fine. My social media displayed a triumphant victory. I'd stuck up well over 1000 posters across the country. Monga Khan was on his way to becoming famous, but something was missing. I thought back to zippole day at Mamma's, when my disagreement with Julian had solidified my plans for Monga Khan. Maybe my obsession with Keith really came down to my unresolved conflict with Julian? I couldn't be sure. It just felt like a tornado inside my head.

Sometimes I receive emails from high school students who want to know about the 'inspiration' for my posters. It's a fair question for which there's never a fair answer. All of my posters begin with a disorganised storm of frustration that won't let me sleep. Then I make something without really knowing why. Then, much later, I convince myself that I knew what I was doing all along. If you asked me why I launched my next poster using a weather balloon in Broken Hill I could probably string a sentence together, but in truth I had no idea what I was doing. All I knew was that I couldn't sleep and I needed to make a new poster that had something to do with family.

Broken Hill

One night, while Julie was sleeping, I stayed up looking through the photos I'd collected from the archive. As raw historical documents they were still so powerful. You could stare straight into the subjects' eyes and they stared right back into you. One person stared into me more than any other. Her name was Wizaree Khalick.

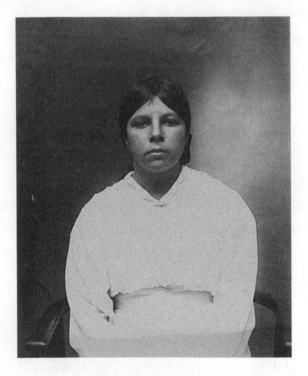

Wizaree was born in Broken Hill but her nationality was listed in the archive as 'British Indian'. The same was true of her brother Abdullah. Their father was Abdul Khalick, who came to Australia in 1880 to work as a cameleer. There was no photo of the children's mother. Their photos appear in the archive because they were travelling to Karachi to meet relatives and to buy camels. Just like the people in the images I'd used for the Aussie posters, these Australian-born kids had requested special exemptions to ensure they wouldn't be denied re-entry into Australia because they weren't white.

Without thinking I took the images of the two children and their father and compiled them into a family photo. I liked the way they looked together. The boy seemed distracted, while the father and daughter's stare looked almost accusing. This was a different image to the heroics of Monga Khan. I added 'AUSSIE' beneath their photo and went to bed.

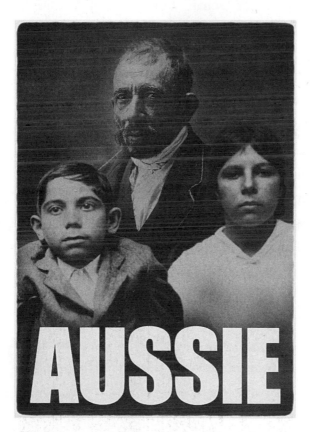

When I woke in the morning I got straight to work. The first thing I did was call my dad. This was to be a poster about family. I wanted my dad's help. I needed my dad's help. There were technical challenges that were beyond my abilities. The plan was to print a series of very large posters, twice the size of the ones I usually make. Using balsa wood and twine, we'd construct a 'kite' to hold three of the posters together in a freestanding, triangular formation. Above the kite we'd inflate large red balloons, the kind used for collecting weather data. We were going to launch the Khalick family atop the Line of Lode Miner's Memorial in Broken Hill. Also, we needed camels.

Within a week we had the oversize printing frame back from the welders. It measured 2.2 metres square. I found a manufacturer in Victoria who could mesh the frame and a commercial printer in Adelaide who could expose it. Using pine and MDF board from Bunnings, I constructed a rig to hold the frame during the printing process. Finally I ordered a 140-centimetre squeegee, and the longest roll of kraft paper on the market. When it all came together in the studio we were ready to print some very large posters. I asked my mate Tomasso to help with the printing. Tom normally prints custom T-shirts, which makes him a perfectionist. I knew his critical eye would offset my stress.

After some initial hiccups the prints came out looking great. We ran off thirty or so, hosed down the screen and packed everything away. The prints were done. Now we just needed some balloons. We also needed those camels.

I wanted to do a test flight, so I bought a tank of helium and a bunch of balloons and drove with Dad out towards Clare, 140 kilometres north of Adelaide. We were well out of any flight path, down a dirt road, surrounded by paddocks. For the next two hours we proceeded to lose our temper with one another as we struggled to build our replica kite out of wood, twine and enormous sheets of paper. It was a shambles, but it came together eventually. The light was fading when we finally released the balloon and it drifted off into the deep blue sky. Only then was I confident it would work. Dad was even happier than I was.

I called Camel Treks Australia. Karen and Paul were based in Hawker and they'd been following the poster project all year. They loved the idea and couldn't wait to be involved. It was Karen who suggested I get in touch with the descendants of cameleers still living in Broken Hill. I made some inquiries and sent out some invitations. The date was set for 10 September, right after I'd be done with Canberra.

I'd timed the event to coincide with the Broken Heel Festival, so I was able to convince a gang of my friends to come along for the ride. Mum and Dad came too. Supporters made the drive from Melbourne and Sydney. Among the crowd that gathered outside the Palace Hotel were the Shamroze family, descendants of the cameleer Shamroze Khan. Some of the locals just came to see the camels.

Dad and I pulled together the kite in the lobby of the hotel before handing it over to the crowd. The balloons twisted wildly in the wind but it somehow held together. Slowly, the crowd and the camels and the kite shuffled down the main street of Broken Hill behind a police escort. It was quite a sight. I had my camera to film the odd parade.

The crowd had halved to about thirty people by the time we reached the top of the Line of Lode. Robert Shamroze said a few words, then we released the balloons and a cheer went up from the crowd. Together we stood and watched it disappear into the infinite expanse. I finally had a chance to chat to the Shamroze clan and Robert invited me to visit the town's mosque.

The following day I interviewed Robert and his son Randell at the Afghan Mosque, a very small building built in 1891 and now a museum where visitors sometimes worship. Randell explained to me how his Australianness is occasionally questioned on the basis of his

appearance. 'I just tell them I'm a descendant of the Australian cam-elecrs,' he said with quiet pride. And then he added with a chuckle, 'I'm not a terrorist.'

Then it was over. The next day I was back in Adelaide.

Even when it was over I didn't know exactly why I'd done it. I was so caught up in getting it done that I didn't give myself time to think. I had told people that it was 'a celebration of the Khalick family' and nobody really asked any questions. I don't blame them. Looking back, it's obvious that I'd deliberately made myself unavailable for discussion. I had to follow it through before I could know what it meant.

It was only when I reviewed the footage and the interviews that it all came together. This wasn't a story of triumph. It had everything to do with alienation and loss. This was the hard truth missing from the pumped-up optimism of Monga Khan. These two Aussie-born kids were denied their sense of belonging in Australia because of the colour of their skin. I couldn't imagine their confusion as they searched for that belonging on the streets of Karachi. All I knew from the records was that Abdullah died aged sixteen, just five years after his photo was taken.

I used my footage and the interviews to create a short film. *The Khalick Family Kite* won Best Documentary at the following year's St Kilda Film Festival. Later I changed its name to *Broken Hill* as it toured festivals in the United States. The film captures the melancholy, but also the resilience. While echoes of the White Australia policy still sound in the prejudices of daily life, people like Randell Shamroze seem able to put that prejudice to shame through proud celebration of the deeds of their ancestors. Does pride in survival dishonour the memory of the oppressed? Not if you're able to tell the whole story. Of course, you can never tell the *whole* story, but you can wage a relentless attempt.

And there you have it, my tidy explanation for why I launched a poster on a weather balloon in Broken Hill. It all came down to another sweeping political metaphor for Australian identity.

Do you feel satisfied? Do you feel that I've been sufficiently open and honest, fulfilling my promise made at the beginning of this book? Well, you shouldn't. At the very least, if you're anything like me, you should be getting a little tired of sweeping political metaphors. Surely I owe you something more. Surely I owe *myself* a deeper explanation. Isn't it a bit suspect that I became so interested in the Khalick family, then the Shamroze family? I have no personal connection to Broken Hill or the cameleers. Why should I care? Why should their family histories be more important to me than my own?

I drove all the way to Broken Hill and back with my parents. That's eleven hours on the road! Eleven hours with the three of us trapped in the same vehicle. Don't you think that might have been a good opportunity for me to bring up our unresolved family history? But why do something like that when I could try to exorcise my own demons by honouring someone else's family? Why should I show courage when I could celebrate someone else's?

That's the real reason I launched that balloon and I'm here to tell you that it didn't work. When I watched that balloon go up and drift across the sky it felt great, but it didn't change a thing. I looked at my dad and he was happy. Together we'd achieved something, but it wasn't the thing we really needed to achieve. I was still furiously groping for that redemption-shaped object, convinced that the darkness was real, oblivious to the fact that my eyes were simply shut.

I can say all this in retrospect. At the time it did feel like progress. I felt that I was deepening my understanding of Australian identity, that I could understand more and more if I simply stretched my arms further to take in everybody else's trauma.

Meanwhile, my own family was trapped. Part of me still believed that I could help my parents, that I could fix their mistakes. If I worked hard enough at something really impressive, maybe they'd have nothing to regret. But the part of me that wanted to abandon their problems was still winning out.

And there were other questions I still hadn't addressed: if our family dysfunction was the root cause of my own weirdness, how had it affected my brothers? How could I help them? How much responsibility did I want to take for it all? That was the key question. At the end of 2016 my answer was 'none'. I would take another two years to find a better answer.

PART THREE

SPIRITUAL
POVERTY

The Racist Publican

I began this book with a promise to describe my difficulty in becoming a man. I said it had everything to do with accepting responsibility and overcoming a kind of spiritual poverty.

Given the political nature of my posters you might be disappointed that I'm aiming at a personal conclusion. That's fair enough. At face value my posters appear to offer simple solutions to large and complex problems. There's something seductive about those broad strokes. There's even some utility in using bold statements to blast through all the muddy nuance and reach out towards an ideal. But without the counterbalance of self-reflection, there's really nothing to stop us from mistaking our personal pathologies for righteous virtues. Ultimately, political art like mine is lacking in self-reflection. Hopefully I can make up for that here.

People my age care a little too much about *identity* and not enough about *character*. My dad once told me a story about character. It wasn't intended that way but that's the way I remember it. It was actually a story about my dad's friend and why my dad didn't trust him. Let's call him Ross Dempsey. Dad loves to repeat stories but he's only told me this story once. Even so, it stands out in my memory.

I would have been about twelve when Dad told it. We had just finished lunch on the back verandah.

'It's a stinking hot day in 1976,' Dad began, 'and we're on a diving trip heading for Port Lincoln when Ross Dempsey and I go into this pub. We walk in, sit down at the bar and order beers, but the bloke behind the bar won't serve us because we're both wearing thongs.'

'Was it a nice-looking pub?' I asked.

'No!' laughed my dad. 'It was ordinary looking. No one there was dressed up. In fact, I could see someone else who was also wearing thongs! So Ross and I think, *This is bullshit*. We tell the bloke, "It's hot. We don't want to put shoes on. We've been driving all day. We're not causing any trouble. We just want a beer." But he still won't serve us. Instead he goes to get the publican.

'By this stage we're thinking this must be some kind of joke. We're two scruffy-looking guys from out of town and this is how the locals make fun of people from the city. But the publican comes in and he's all apologies. He says, "So sorry about the misunderstanding, fellas, we're happy to have ya. It's just that we need to maintain some kind of standard, otherwise the next thing you know there'll be Abos in here."

'I stand up and say, "We're not drinking here," but Ross just acts like it's no big deal!' Dad shook his head with an expression of disappointment, bordering on contempt. 'That was Ross Dempsey.'

I remember the surprise I felt when I heard this story. I remember the feeling of a new rule clicking into place: *When someone says something racist, don't stand for it. That's what Dad does. That's what you should do.* It's that simple when you're young and you want to be like your dad. I couldn't wait to grow up and live in Dad's world, where a man's actions decide his character.

The rest of my dad's stories are all about mischief and glory. There was the time he and his mates at teacher's college attached a gelignite fuse to a giant balloon of oxy-acetylene gas. The balloon floated off into the night sky and exploded with enough force to wake the entire town of Meningie. 'Everyone knew we'd done it,' whispered Dad with glee, 'but they couldn't prove it.' More edifying stories came in the form of discovering shipwrecks and recovering artefacts from the ocean floor. We'd visit maritime museums and see the exhibits that Dad had helped to build. My dad was my hero. In the schoolyard I would say, 'My dad has swum with whales and found shipwrecks,' and the other kids would always be impressed. Dad made great efforts to encourage us to take up scuba diving but I couldn't because I had asthma. I knew I'd find some other means of adventure.

Now that I think of it, Dad has a couple of other stories that don't fit under the category of mischief and glory. I'm talking about the stories where Dad got hurt, where somebody hurt my dad. I was once walking with him down Grenfell Street in the city and two men were walking towards us. One of them looked at Dad and said his name. My dad returned the stare and said the man's name, but we just kept walking. Then he turned to me and said, 'That was the student who broke my nose when I was teaching at Elizabeth.' The student had punched Dad in the face, crushing his upper lateral cartilage and leaving him with the boxer's nose he has today.

At the same school, Dad had stood in a picket line when the teachers went on strike, only to have a scab drive his car into Dad's legs, busting his knee. Later he discovered that the union had made a deal before the strike even started. The strike was just for show, so Dad's busted knee was for nothing.

If he'd left us, I might not have heard any of Dad's stories. I value those stories. More than any of the books I've read, artworks I've seen or movies I've watched, those stories give me a little picture of my place in the world and how I should act.

I have one more story from him that's worth telling. Dad's father was a dressmaker. He ran a workshop that made clothes for Myer as well as military uniforms during the war. One day, when Dad was in primary school, all the students were asked to bring in an object for a show-and-tell about what their fathers did for work. My dad brought an iron. Not an electric iron; this was a cast iron. Small but heavy.

On the tram home from school, an older boy made fun of my dad. 'Ironing, that's women's work,' he said, but Dad just ignored him. The taunting continued. 'Sounds to me like you've got two mums,' the boy said. Dad stayed silent. The older boy got off the tram with my dad and still the taunting continued. Then, when the older boy wasn't looking, Dad held his schoolbag by its straps and swung it round his body like an Olympic hammer thrower. The boy went down hard. The weight of the iron made all the difference. Luckily the boy wasn't seriously injured. He never bothered Dad again.

Whenever my dad told that story it always made him a little bit sad. For a long time I didn't understand why. When I was a kid I just wanted to hear how the bully got what he deserved. Instead, Dad made me feel sorry for the bully. He didn't like encouraging us to use violence, but he didn't forbid it either. Knowing when and how much violence took *character*. Pretty quickly I understood that the threat of violence is the bedrock to all authority. If you don't understand that, someone else is understanding it for you.

However, there's one category of stories that's missing from my Dad's catalogue. I've never heard the stories where my Dad really did the wrong thing, where he hurt someone else who simply didn't deserve it. He must have those stories. Everyone's hurt people when they shouldn't have. I feel like I'm old enough to hear those stories. I want to know what not to do. I want to know what I'll regret. I want to hear a story about doing the wrong thing and finding forgiveness. When you're a child your parents are there to forgive you, but who forgives you when your parents are gone? Who's going to forgive the racist publican? Who's going to forgive Australia – God? I once asked my mum about God.

'Mum, is God real?' I said.

'What do you think?' was her only reply.

Australia Day

By the end of 2016 I was twice as exhausted as the previous year but no more fulfilled. I'd come to realise that it's impossible to tell a sufficient amount of truth in any one poster, but if I pushed ahead, uncovering more boundaries, maybe I could still find that feeling of transformation I'd set out to discover in the first place. By evoking the theme of Australian identity, I felt I'd obligated myself to produce a complete picture of Australia. So what pieces were missing from my picture? Alone in my studio, I went back to the beginning to inspect those lines from the anthem that had inspired it all. Very quickly, I found something ...

> We've boundless plains to share ...

Really? It seems a little hyperbolic to claim that the Australian landmass is 'boundless'. Maybe our anthem's fondness for superlatives betrays the dubious methods with which the land was acquired? To an ear attuned to history, maybe our anthem sounds more like the spruiking of a street vendor as he tries to offload stolen goods? But I didn't want to go there. Who does? Wouldn't we all rather just get on with our lives and leave the most difficult aspects of history to someone else? After all, if we do a complete audit of human history we might find that none of us are innocent. Perhaps we're all complicit. Perhaps that's the secular version of original sin.

With these, and other, confusing questions, I shied away from my initial impulse to address Australia's legacy of colonisation. With the end of the year approaching, it seemed like a good time to focus my attention on my personal life. If my little outburst in Brisbane revealed anything, it was the possibility that there were still unresolved resentments lurking deep inside my own personality. Maybe I should iron out those kinks before heading off on another foolhardy crusade to fix everyone else's problems.

On Christmas Day, Julie and I went to my parents' house for dinner.

We all got along fine as long as we didn't talk about anything meaningful. Instead we talked about the cats.

'Oh, look at Mr Fluffy! Isn't he gorgeous?' said Dad.

In defence of Mr Fluffy, he really was a beautiful cat, but not quite beautiful enough to distract from the fact that Simon was wearing a MAGA cap. Trump had won the US presidential election a month prior and Simon was delighting in the absurdity of being the only gay man in Australia who would have voted for the orange narcissist given the chance. Julian stayed in his room. He'd emerged earlier to accept his gifts but saw that as the extent of his familial obligations.

'Where's Sweet Pea?' asked Mum without any real interest. Sweet Pea was preening in the lounge.

Simon kept sneaking off to his room to fill his cup with something strong. I didn't realise what was happening until his speech slowed right down and he started repeating himself. He was too drunk to realise that he wasn't getting away with it. Being around him when he's drunk just reminds me of being punched. It was time to leave.

On the drive home I gave up on finding solace by resolving my family conflict. I didn't exactly know what I wanted from them but I felt sure I wasn't going to get it. The task of untangling Australia's identity suddenly seemed more feasible. On Boxing Day I returned to my studio, determined to find an idea that would get me back on that wave of public enthusiasm.

I was sketching ideas for new posters when my memory bumped over something that had happened much earlier in the year. I'd been invited to attend a protest to disrupt the official Australia Day parade on King William Street in Adelaide. *Why not?* I thought, expecting a monocultural parade of hateful bogans. But when I arrived I discovered the opposite – a multicultural kaleidoscope of newly naturalised Australians from all over the world. Thousands of people were celebrating while thirty or so protesters were psyching themselves up on the sidelines, preparing to 'disrupt'. I couldn't join them. I wasn't interested in shouting at confused immigrants, but I couldn't leave either. I just found a place to sit and watch the conflict unfold.

I wondered why so few of the protesters were Aboriginal, but I didn't wonder for long. Only privileged white kids can muster the moral vanity required to appropriate the outrage of Aboriginal people, believing that they are addressing the legacy of dispossession by scaring a bunch of immigrants on Australia Day.

'*Always was, always will be, Aboriginal land! Always was, always will be, Aboriginal land!*'

I usually liked that chant, but not that day. As the protesters grew louder, they locked arms and moved in to block the road. With the parade halted, the protesters' chant roared even louder, but then everything got quiet and awkward.

The protesters had found themselves face to face with the Muslim Women's Association of South Australia – not exactly the enemy they'd been hoping for. The women held their confused children closer as they attempted to find a way around. Even the protesters were visibly conflicted. That changed when the police arrived. Suddenly they felt much better. The chanting returned to full volume as they clashed with police and the press photographers arrived right on cue.

The protest was a dishonest spectacle, but so were the official celebrations. Using multiculturalism to distract from the crushing effects of colonisation seems disingenuous, especially since you could easily celebrate multiculturalism on any other date. But most Australians would rather stay connected to Britain than truly take responsibility for our history. So Australian identity remains stuck, while Aboriginal identity is forced to degenerate into a politicised shadow of itself, dependent upon its opposition to 'whiteness'. Clearly Aboriginal identity is more than that. Clearly Australia is more than just a British colony. So why can't we move beyond what is clearly a lose-lose situation?

How could I express all that in a poster? I had a feeling that I couldn't, but I didn't care. I was going to try. I was going to push ahead because I'd already come too far to stop.

Real Australians Seek Welcome

The new year arrived on a wave of hysteria. Somehow, Donald Trump had won the US election. On 20 January 2017 he was inaugurated. After eight years of Americans patting themselves on the back for electing a black president, they now had to admit that their post-racial utopia had been a fantasy. The shockwaves of disillusionment rippled around the world. All that energy had to go somewhere and it quickly became the fuel for movements promising social change. This was boom time for counter-culture.

The real action was happening on the battlefield of gender politics. The worldwide Women's March, on the day after Trump's inauguration, lit the fuse that would explode into the #metoo movement later that year. This was the year of compulsory feminism. As a white, middle-class male I saw no room for my participation. My role was to shut up and listen. Unfortunately posters don't listen, so I turned away from the spectacle of the moment and recommitted to addressing Australia's colonial legacy.

Before the year began it was clear that the government-funded 'Recognise' campaign was failing to attract the broad support it needed. Since 2012 the campaign had been raising awareness of the need to change the Australian constitution to acknowledge the Indigenous presence. Everyone agreed that Australia needed a referendum on this, but the 'Recognise' campaign didn't go far enough. It seemed many Aboriginal leaders wanted structural reform, not just symbolic change.

I wanted to avoid getting caught up in the big fight. I really just wanted to make a small statement of my own, off to the side where nobody was looking. If I could hit upon a useful insight, maybe I could contribute something relatively uncontroversial, then slowly back away from the whole 'Australian identity' thing.

My starting point was the perverse spectacle I'd witnessed the year before, when anti-Australia Day protesters clashed with newly naturalised migrants. Surely these two groups weren't really enemies? Surely they needed to act as allies if reconciliation was the goal. *Was* reconciliation still the goal? I assumed so. Ever since primary school I'd been hearing about reconciliation. Whenever the teacher read us an Aboriginal Dreaming story we were reminded that we all had to 'work together for reconciliation'. Everyone seemed to be on board, so why were those wounds still open? What was missing from the reconciliation process?

These were the questions I was asking myself as I sat in the studio sketching ideas for the project. The first design came easily. I liked the way it presented the inverse of the original poster. I hoped that together they conveyed the paradox at the core of Australia's identity.

However, on its own, 'Real Australians Seek Welcome' was too ambiguous. The casual passer-by might not catch its meaning. It had to be more direct, so I designed this:

But still, this poster hardly said anything new. We all know Australia was built on Aboriginal land, and acknowledging that fact is a well-established cultural practice. I really wanted to make a statement addressing the conflict I'd seen between protesters and migrants on Australia Day. Surely Australian multiculturalism is something we're all proud of? Maybe I could put forward the idea that Aboriginality was at the core of Australian multiculturalism. I started writing what would become the script for the project's launch video.

> Hello, my name's Peter Drew and for the last two years I've
> been sticking up thousands of posters all over Australia that
> celebrate our multiculturalism. But what are the origins of
> Australian multiculturalism? Before Europeans invaded, this
> island continent was home to upwards of 250 distinct
> language groups, each with their own customs and culture.

One custom was to acknowledge other groups' traditional ownership and to seek welcome in those lands. So this year I've designed a new poster. Actually, I've designed 250 new posters, one for every language group, and I need your help making sure they get to where they belong. I'm going to be travelling to all the capital cities sticking up 1000 posters across the country, but I need volunteers in all the remaining areas … Ultimately this project celebrates the origins of Australia's multiculturalism, but in reality it's about our future. Today fewer than 150 Aboriginal languages remain in daily use. So what we're really talking about is 60,000 years of cultural survival and that's something that we can all admire and learn from.

Was the diversity of Aboriginal culture *really* the origin of Australia's multiculturalism? I could see good arguments for and against the notion, but it did seem like a powerful rhetorical tool for evoking a potential continuity between modern Australia and the deep history of the First Peoples.

I made a few calculations and figured I'd need to raise $13,000 to print and distribute 250 separate designs, as well as travel to the capital cities and stick up posters myself. This was a vast miscalculation – not only of the project's popularity and my consequent ability to raise funds, but also of the costs inherent in its execution. However, the real problem was the concept.

Over the next six months my project would unravel under the weight of its own ambition. I was completely unprepared for the realities of the political landscape I was entering. Naivety had never stopped me in the past, but this time was different.

Launch

I put a call out on social media asking for volunteers to be in the campaign video. For the previous two years I'd been the only person speaking in my videos, but for this project I knew I had to place the audience front and centre. I was planning to make one of those painfully sincere videos where the camera cuts between multiple people reading the same script in front of a neutral backdrop, while staring down the lens with an earnest expression. I hate those videos. I can't stand the conceit of presenting a multitude of people who apparently think in unison, but that's what I was planning to do.

It was a very hot day when the volunteers showed up for the shoot at Tooth & Nail Studio. It was a diverse group of about forty people. I handed everyone a script and asked them to read it over. Only then did they discover the project's concept. Anyone who was unsure about it could leave. No one left. One volunteer suggested a minor adjustment to the script, but that was all. The only paid actor was Natasha Wanganeen. I asked her to go first, and she made it look easy, giving everyone else a little more confidence. Also, the fact that Natasha was Indigenous surely helped the whiteys feel less hesitant to speak. The biggest problem was the heat. Tooth & Nail was a tin hotbox packed full of people. It took almost three hours to get through everyone. There were many pauses to wipe away sweat.

I launched the project on 23 January, amid the annual conflict that precedes Australia Day. It garnered considerable attention in the press but not the level of support I'd anticipated. It didn't catch fire like the previous two projects. I wasn't surprised – in the days before the launch I'd been extremely nervous and felt little confidence in the project's success. I thought it was too complicated, too ambitious and too ambiguous. How exactly should real Australians 'seek welcome'? I doubted whether the posters themselves carried the point about multiculturalism. Actually, I knew they didn't. But I pressed on with the project regardless, because I felt I had to keep moving, if not to succeed then at least to understand my mistakes.

Because the project failed to spread virally I resorted to advertising, which quickly ate into my budget. The crowdfunding campaign needed to reach its full target of $13,000, otherwise I'd receive no funding at all. As the weeks passed and support for the project slowly grew, I tried to focus on getting the posters printed.

A week after launching the project I received a concerned email from someone at the Australian Institute of Aboriginal and Torres Strait Islander Studies, the organisation that publishes the Aboriginal language map I'd referenced in the campaign. It stated:

> One thing you should be aware of is the map you are using,
> in some regions, such as with the Yorta Yorta, for example, is
> contested. We are undergoing a project to review the map as
> it is highly useful but was created a long time ago and
> contains some inaccuracies and the evidence base for some
> of the assumptions of boundaries sometimes varies.

I hadn't even considered that possibility. What if I stuck up a poster in a contested area? Wouldn't that be stirring up needless conflict? Maybe I could simply stick to the uncontested areas – but where were they? I could say goodbye to my free-range postering style. I'd need to add an extra layer of research before I even cooked my glue. I took a deep breath and tried to remind myself, *This is what you wanted, a long, slow campaign that goes deeper than ever.* I'd never felt this way before. This was the first time I could remember really doubting my own project before I'd even begun.

Permission

A few people suggested that I seek permission to use the names of the Aboriginal language groups. I've never sought permission to use a word, so I was initially sceptical. Surely my posters fit within the custom of 'Acknowledgement of Country', which is an established cultural norm for non-Aboriginal Australians? *Who exactly owns these words?* I thought. Could I ask permission from anyone who spoke that language? Probably not. Perhaps I needed to seek permission from elders. But isn't direct communication between artist and audience the whole point of street art? And what about young Indigenous people who aren't elders? Why couldn't I seek *their* permission? I decided that the safest thing to do was to start making inquiries.

I contacted someone I'd worked with previously at an Aboriginal arts organisation. She said she 'absolutely loved' the project and was happy to put me in touch with Uncle Sam Diamond for permission to use the Kaurna name. *Great!* I thought. All I had to do was reach out and things would fall into place. I could repeat the process for every poster design around the country. I didn't care how long it might take. But after a couple of weeks without a reply from Uncle Sam, I decided to go back to my contact. She knew another Uncle, Mitch Gabris. He was the son of a respected Kaurna elder. 'He's expecting your call,' she said. I was excited to get started.

We met at a café in the city, but from the outset I knew it wasn't going to unfold as I had hoped. Mitch wouldn't look me in the eye. I'd brought along a poster to show him what the project was all about but he didn't want to see it. Instead we sat down and he explained to me the importance of culture to his people.

'Yes, that's why I'm here,' I said. 'To ask permission to use the Kaurna name. The aim of this project is to celebrate that culture.'

'But it's not yours to celebrate,' said Mitch. He opened a folder that he'd brought with him. It was filled with photos of his people. 'You tell me,' he said. 'Do *you* look like this? Or this, or this?' Until then he'd been sullen but now he was letting out his anger. Now he was looking straight at me.

'Okay, I get it,' I said. 'I'm not Aboriginal but I thought this meeting was set up so I could ask permission to use the word.'

'The answer's no,' said Mitch. 'You people think you can take everything, but this is ours. It's our culture, and you can't have it.'

I leaned back and let out a long breath. 'Can I ask you one question?' I said. 'Because I'm still having trouble understanding. You've been doing this a long time, right? This isn't the first time a white person has come to you asking permission to use the Kaurna name?'

'I've been doing this for ten years,' said Mitch, still looking me straight in the eye. 'I've had dozens of your people come to me, doing what you're doing.'

'And how many times have you said yes?'

'Never. None!' said Mitch. 'I've never let any whitefella use the Kaurna name.'

I realised that I'd been brought here to be taught a lesson. It had never been a discussion. I looked up at the ceiling and let out a big sigh.

'What, you think this is funny?' he said.

'Yeah, I do think it's funny,' I said. 'I came here thinking I had a chance but now I understand that it's not worth asking. What's yours is yours and what's mine is mine, and that's that.'

'Except, what's yours isn't yours,' said Mitch. 'You're sleeping on stolen land, my people's land. How's that yours?'

'You're preaching to the choir, mate. Do you really think I'd make this poster if I didn't already understand that?' I pleaded, one last time.

'You *cannot* use the Kaurna name,' Mitch said finally.

'Oh, I hear ya,' I said, and stood up to leave.

I stuck out my hand and Mitch shook it reluctantly. As I walked to my car I wondered whether I'd been set up. Hadn't my contact at the arts organisation 'absolutely loved' the project? Why would she send me to a guy like Mitch, who never grants permission?

By the time I'd arrived home I'd decided that I didn't care. Now that I'd asked for permission and been rejected I couldn't continue with the project as I'd originally planned. I simply decided to stop using any of the Aboriginal names. I would revert to using the original 'Aboriginal Land' poster and leave it at that.

Only later was I offered an explanation for the rejection. I was told by email that because I'd already printed the posters and distributed them to several institutions, I had broken the rules. That was the reason Mitch was upset. It didn't ring true to me. Mitch hadn't mentioned anything of the sort. Besides, one of the institutions where I'd distributed the posters was the Aboriginal arts organisation itself, at its request! But by that stage I'd already given up.

I announced my decision to withdraw on social media, and immediately right-wing followers took the opportunity to gloat. The lefties jumped in to remind me that I was white and should just keep quiet. They fought it out in the comments section. It was just as constructive as you might imagine. However, some good did come of it. I received several messages from Aboriginal leaders who urged me to keep going. One was from a Kaurna man who'd already received one of my posters. He offered to meet.

I'd first met Sam when he did the Welcome to Country at an event I attended. I was struck then by his warmth and generosity. It was a relief to see him again. Something about his stocky build and thick beard reminded me of my dad. We met at a city café during his lunch-break, and I told him about what had happened with Mitch. He seemed to understand before I'd even finished.

'You did it wrong,' said Sam. 'There's a proper way to ask permission from elders and you've got to go through the right channels. Mitch isn't an elder so I don't know why you were sent to him, but that's not important. What matters is that you do it right from now on.'

I agreed, and Sam took me to meet his dad, who is a Kaurna elder. I showed him the poster and explained the overall concept. It took about three minutes. Sam's dad saw no problem and, with that out of the way, he proceeded to tell me the history of his people for the next hour. It was like standing under a waterfall. 'People don't realise,' he kept saying, before throwing down yet another piece of knowledge about the land I thought I knew. My head was spinning but I didn't want it to end.

I went home feeling overwhelmed. I'd come into the project knowing that it was a fraught landscape, filled with good and bad actors alike, but I hadn't really questioned the possibility that I would lack the political fortitude for the necessary negotiations. The one thing I did know for sure is I had fundamental disagreements with participating in a system that guarded culture within racial boundaries. I understand the impulse to protect but I don't think it works. In the long term I think it has the opposite effect. By imposing a false sense of vulnerability, culture tends to grow more dependent upon its protectors. But those boundaries aren't really mine to break. Ultimately it's up to Aboriginal artists to express their own frustration in having their work defined within racial boundaries, and plenty do.

I decided to stick with my decision to abandon further use of the Aboriginal language groups. By the time I pulled the plug I still had enough funds to travel and stick up some 'Aboriginal Land' posters. After all the back-and-forth negotiations, I couldn't wait to get back on the street.

So What?

It was June before I stuck up a single poster. As I stepped out of the Sydney Central YHA in the pre-dawn light with a bag full of posters and a bucket full of glue, I thought, *What have I been waiting for?* This was what it was all about for me: an excuse to assault the urban landscape with my posters.

I'm always nervous when I put up a new design. As I unfurl the poster I like to imagine a bystander shouting, 'What the fuck!' Their hands are over their head to prevent their mind from exploding. Of course it never happens, and that particular morning in Sydney was a strikingly low-key event. I stuck up the 'Aboriginal Land' poster on its own and also in a set of three. I liked the way it looked as a set. As the dawn light rose the rain started to fall and the streets filled with people who ignored my posters on their way to work. I pressed on.

In Darlington I found an old poster of Monga Khan that had actually improved with age. All the others were in need of replacement. After a few hours cleaning up my old work and occasionally adding new posters, I felt more like a gardener than any kind of rebel. It felt good. All over Sydney I found weather-beaten posters of Monga Khan that I lovingly replaced. Several times I attracted appreciative comments from passers-by, but when I stuck up the 'Aboriginal Land' posters they attracted barely any attention.

Well, this is nice, I thought as I went about my business. All the rage that had propelled my previous projects seemed to have melted away. As a result I was far less productive. *What's the point of getting blisters on your feet? The streets will still be there tomorrow! Take a rest. Answer some emails. That's work too.*

On the street I was less aggressive. It's very easy to stick up posters and not get caught if you simply stick to the safe spots. In the past I'd pushed myself to hit the hard spots, the impossible spots. It's a great feeling sticking up a poster in broad daylight on the headquarters of a multinational corporation. It's a great feeling getting away with it by timing your attack to coincide with a delivery truck that blocks the security cameras. It's a thrill. You get a little ego boost with every conquest. But this time around I just wasn't feeling the need.

On my last day in Sydney I'd planned to focus on the downtown area. I knew plenty of easy spots and felt sure I could find some new ones. Counterintuitively, crowded areas are often the easiest places to stick up posters because everyone's sense of personal responsibility is diluted.

My favourite spot in the whole city is near the intersection of George and Bond streets. There's an awful grey wall that faces south, so all the foot traffic coming up George Street is forced to stare at it. I climbed onto the electricity box at the foot of the wall and stuck an 'Aboriginal Land' poster as high as I could. It was the last spot of the day and I was feeling good. But as I hopped down, a guy about my age in a suit looked me right in the eye and said 'So what?' as he walked past without pausing.

I'd never had a reaction that was quite so casually dismissive. I was a little taken aback, so I packed up my gear and took off my hi-vis vest and anonymously watched people's reactions for a while. There was a steady stream of about fifty people a minute coming up George Street. Maybe one in ten looked up at the poster. Every now and then

someone would roll their eyes. No one looked surprised. They'd heard
the message before. 'Aboriginal Land ... no shit!' they seemed to say.

The longer I stayed the more disappointed I felt. I didn't particularly mind that my old posters had become part of the scenery, but my
new design wasn't even interesting to begin with. It didn't provoke
any new thoughts. It wasn't a catalyst for change. It just seemed to
land on that place in people's mind where hypocrisy is shrugged off
and forgotten.

But wasn't this what I wanted? Hadn't I deliberately set out to
achieve something 'off to the side' and 'uncontroversial'? I was

beginning to realise that it wasn't much of an achievement. The graffiti kid in me wasn't satisfied. What was the point of assaulting the urban landscape if the passers-by felt nothing? I'd been in Sydney for a full week. I was just as exhausted as I'd been the previous two years. I'd covered a vast amount of territory. But the most fun I'd had was repairing old posters. The 'Aboriginal Land' design had no fire in it, and I realised I wasn't okay with that. I wanted to know what I'd missed. I needed help to understand.

Apologise!

The pattern continued in Melbourne. I set up shop in the YHA on Flinders Street and spent most of my time replacing damaged posters across the city. I'll admit that the 'Aboriginal Land' poster did receive a positive reception in Hosier Lane, but that's hardly an achievement. People go to Hosier Lane to take wedding photos with murals of celebrities. Elsewhere in Melbourne the poster attracted the same indifference as it had in Sydney.

I had an old guy tear down one of my fresh Monga Khan posters early one morning in Footscray, but that was pretty ordinary. What made his reaction odd was that he ignored a nearby 'Aboriginal Land' poster and went straight for Monga Khan. Once he was gone I simply retrieved the torn poster from the ground and stuck it back up again. I was left wondering what made Monga Khan so provocative. Or, more to the point, why didn't anyone seem to care about 'Seeking Welcome' on Aboriginal Land?

Late one night I was back on the Melbourne University campus, happily postering the Morris columns when I finally encountered someone with a strong reaction. I heard a sound behind me and turned to see a man in his early twenties. He was filming me on his phone as he stood about five metres away. Before I could say anything he commenced the interrogation.

'Peter Drew, when will you apologise for your disrespect of Indigenous culture?'

There was an awkward pause.

'How's that?' I said, looking him up and down. It's impossible to describe him accurately without evoking the stereotype. This guy was covered in all the latest accoutrements of wokeness. Coloured hair, piercings and esoteric tattoos were just the beginning. Even his posture suggested a kind of limp superiority. His pallid complexion completed the cliché. I had a sudden urge to eat a steak. This guy was beyond white; he was transparent, in every sense. He was also safe behind his camera. In the video he was making, it was just me against his anonymous accusations.

'When will you apologise for appropriating Indigenous culture? When will you apologise for your attempts to exploit Indigenous culture for the rehabilitation of the very structures that profit from dispossession, mass incarceration and genocide?' he said with impressive speed.

'You mean Australia?' I asked. 'You want me to apologise to you, for Australia? That's just fucking ridiculous.' I turned back to my poster. It was almost done. Just a couple more licks of glue and I'd have no more reason to stick around. But I didn't want to leave. Part of me was arrogant enough to believe that I could turn this guy around. I heard him step closer before he repeated his accusation.

'When will you apologise to elders, past and present, for your attempts to rehabilitate Australia's white supremacy?'

'Don't you think you might be overstating that just a little?' I said, still facing my work. 'Besides, shouldn't demands for an apology come with the possibility of forgiveness? You don't seem like you're interested in forgiveness.'

He took another step closer.

'When will you apologise to elders, past and present, for your attempts to rehabilitate Australia's white supremacy?' he tried for the last time.

'You seem like a nice guy,' I said, 'but I'm just not ready for that level of commitment. We can still fuck, obviously, but no kissing, okay?'

There was a pause. I had finished gluing the poster three times over, so I turned to face him.

'When will —' he started, but I cut him off.

'I should tell you, I have herpes,' I said. 'Full-blown genital herpes ... I don't have a break-out right now, but you should still wear a condom.'

He didn't even blink. He just kept looking at me through his phone as the silence stretched out between us.

'Yeah, well, I've got AIDS,' he spat out with a smirk, before spinning around and walking away faster than I could think.

I stood dumbfounded under the lamplight, watching him disappear into the night. He'd outdone me at my own game. A big grin crept across my face as I wondered whether I'd ever again meet someone so completely at ease with their own absurdity. I was almost disappointed when the video failed to surface on the internet. Actually, that's not true. The last thing I want is for anybody to know I have herpes.

For the rest of my time in Melbourne I couldn't stop thinking about my friend with AIDS. He made me wonder, who else out there was playing a character? Maybe I was playing a character? I didn't think so, but how could I be sure? Maybe if I spoke to someone else who was playing a character, someone who seemed to be operating out of bad faith just to amuse themselves, maybe then I would understand myself better. One name immediately sprang to mind.

Opportunity Makes the Thief

I tracked down the address of Keith's office with a little help from a friend. I'd assumed that someone like him would have a grand office in one of Melbourne's most intimidating towers, so I was surprised to discover that he'd opted for a little old building down the east end of Collins Street. I sent him an email with a light-hearted request for a meeting but received no reply. It was my last day in Melbourne so I thought, *What the hell? I'll just show up at his door and see what happens.*

After a morning of postering I caught the number 11 tram to see him. I'd left all my gear at the hostel and put on some semi-clean clothes. As I stood on the tram I tried to formulate a plan for what I would say, but quickly realised I had no idea. All I knew about Keith was that he sometimes worked for a conservative think tank, the name of which I couldn't even remember. On both our previous meetings he seemed to relish the opportunity to mock my posters and everything they stood for. That's why I felt confident he would agree to see me. I had a feeling that men like Keith take pleasure in dissecting other men. To him, I was easy prey. But I wasn't scared. After two weeks of being ignored on the street I was looking forward to it.

I took myself up the stairs and searched the rabbit warren of narrow corridors for Keith's office. The place was full of small law and accounting practices. Apart from the herringbone wood floors, the interior was very plain. I found the door I was looking for. I hesitated. Then I knocked and a female voice said, 'Come in.'

'Hello,' I said, stepping in. 'I'm here to see Keith. I don't have an

appointment but I was hoping to get his opinion on my new design.'
I held up the single rolled poster I'd brought with me.

'Oh, yes, okay,' said the elderly secretary with a mixture of warmth and confusion. She asked my name and told me to sit down before she stepped out. From the next room I could hear her speaking quietly. Then I heard Keith let out a chuckle. A second later he appeared, wearing his most conspiratorial smile.

'Drew, what a pleasant surprise! Come in. Thank you, Grace.'

Keith's office was lined with cheap shelves that were filled with binders, and one antique shelf filled with books I didn't recognise. His desk was an oak rectangle with a green leather top and matching chairs. He even had one of those green desk lamps amid the clutter. The office was small and cramped. The only things in the room that didn't obviously relate to work were the books and a large print of Max Dupain's 'Sunbaker' that hung on the wall behind Keith's desk.

'You like Max Dupain?' I asked.

'It's a powerful image,' said Keith curtly. 'How can I help?'

'I'm sorry to bother you at work but I was hoping to get your opinion on my new poster,' I said.

'Let me guess, climate change?' Keith quipped.

'Colonisation, actually.' I stood up to unfurl the poster.

'No, not in here,' Keith protested. 'Why not just tell me about it?'

So I sat down and told Keith all about the design. I told him how my original plan had fallen apart and how people on the street seemed unmoved by the 'Aboriginal Land' poster. I told him that I didn't know why.

'Well, that's easy,' said Keith. 'Because everybody understands that opportunity makes the thief.'

'What do you mean?'

Keith leaned forward. 'Do you honestly believe that anyone in this country doesn't already realise that this was once Aboriginal land? From a young age, every Australian student is told "respect the traditional owners", etcetera, etcetera. We all know the land was seized, we're just too polite to say so.'

'I wouldn't call that politeness,' I said.

'No? You don't think Aborigines are ashamed of the fact they couldn't prevent the land from being taken? Of course they are. The word "settlement" is simply a polite compromise between "invasion" and "conquest". It allows Aborigines to forget they were conquered and it allows the rest of us to forget about our own brutality.'

'I'm not sure it's working,' I said. 'I mean, you seem pretty comfortable with accepting that brutality. Wouldn't we all be better off if we acknowledged the truth?'

Keith leaned far back in his chair. 'No,' he said eventually. 'All of the most beautiful things created by man were made in compensation for the truth. That's why nobody likes your ghastly poster!' He let out a short laugh, as if he'd surprised himself.

'Well, I'm glad I came here,' I said, 'because it's making it easier to take you less seriously. Do you even believe what you're saying?'

'Why not?' said Keith, still amused. But he could see that he was losing me. 'I apologise,' he said. 'You've been polite to me, so I should return the favour. But let me ask you this – how much culture from 1788 remains alive today, and how much has been swept aside by modernity? Can you dance an Irish jig or recite the Lord's Prayer? Can you milk a cow or sow a field?'

I shook my head.

'Of course you can't. But nobody puts pressure on you to look backwards and bemoan all that you've supposedly lost, because white people are allowed to believe in progress. Now, consider all the pressure placed upon the Aborigine to "be Aboriginal" and perform the cruel pantomime of a culture set in opposition to modernity, just to service our delusion of sensitivity. Consider the cost of that delusion. Australia spends billions every year simply maintaining the shocking disadvantage of remote communities. We could start to "close the gap" tomorrow if we took the steps necessary to encourage those communities to assimilate, economically and socially. But that would require us to surrender the idea of the world's "oldest living culture", artificially kept frozen in time. Maybe we're so greedy that we think we can be powerful as well as innocent? Or maybe we're just afraid that we won't be forgiven for what it took to create modern Australia?'

Keith wasn't smiling anymore. After a pause he continued.

'It's no wonder we tell ourselves stories of a unifying spirit and write noble documents. Maybe it's the best we can do to legislate our base natures into civility.'

He seemed spent, like he'd said what he really wanted to say, but regretted it. I actually felt sorry for him because he seemed to grasp that the answers he was seeking were probably beyond his own understanding. I didn't feel up to putting him on the spot, so I changed the subject.

'Why do you like that image?' I asked, looking up at the Sunbaker behind him. Keith turned to look at it and a weary smile returned to his face.

'I don't know,' he said. 'Maybe for all the reasons that I don't necessarily agree with everything I just told you.'

'What do you mean?' I said, suddenly alert.

But Keith looked me straight in the eye and said, 'No. Now, unless you're in a position to open an account, I'm going to have to ask you to leave.' His smile was gone.

I stood up. He rose also and stuck out his hand. I shook it, picked up my poster and got out of there. A minute later I was back on Collins Street among the normal people knocking off from work. I found a café and wrote down everything that Keith had said, as best as I could remember it. I knew he'd said more than he'd intended to. I knew I'd never get that chance again, but I felt like I'd heard more than enough. Any time I didn't feel like getting out of bed to stick up posters, any time I didn't want to cook up another batch of glue, any time I felt like giving up, I could always read what Keith had said and find all the motivation I needed to keep going.

The Trolley Problem

I knew I didn't agree with what Keith had said, but I couldn't say why. His opinions weren't the kind you can easily confront without being sucked into their vortex of self-loathing and brutality. They seemed like the kind of opinions you need to tunnel underneath. I had a feeling that something was missing right at the core of Keith's worldview and I needed time to figure out what it was. In the meantime, his dislike of my current poster was encouraging.

After Melbourne I joined a group of friends who were heading to Tasmania for the Dark Mofo festival. We were splitting the cost of accommodation so I'd be able to see the festival at night and put up posters in the morning. The chance to be immersed in other people's art seemed like the break I needed.

Apparently I wasn't the only one. Every year half a million contemporary art fans turn mid-winter Hobart into a theme park for the disillusioned. The whole town gets coloured black and red. It's about as edgy as a goth kid's twenty-first birthday party, yet it manages to pull $50 million into the city's economy. Every year there's a controversy and in 2017 it was a performance art piece by Hermann Nitsch, for which a bull would be taken off the feedlot and ritually sacrificed for art. Naturally, my gut reaction was to side with the artist. My other gut reaction was disgust. Nitsch's work is deliberately repulsive. I had no interest in seeing people covered in animal blood. However, I greatly enjoyed the controversy leading up to the festival.

I especially enjoyed David Walsh's personal contribution to the debate. He issued a good-humoured statement on MONA's website, exploring the positive, though unintended, consequences of horrific acts. He cited the Port Arthur massacre and the subsequent change to gun laws that saved hundreds of lives. He then went on to invoke the thought experiment known as the 'trolley problem':

> There is a runaway trolley barrelling down the railway tracks. Ahead, on the tracks, there are five people tied up and unable to move. The trolley is headed straight for them. You are standing some distance off, next to a lever. If you pull this lever, the trolley will switch to a different set of tracks. However, you notice that there is one person on the side track. You have two options:
>
> 1. Do nothing, and the trolley kills the five people on the main track.
> 2. Pull the lever, diverting the trolley onto the side track where it will kill one person.
>
> Which is the most ethical choice?
>
> ... Most people pull the lever. They kill one to save five. So the ends justify the means? Not so fast. When the experiment is slightly altered, so that one has to push a fat man onto the tracks to stop the trolley, very few will do it ... It is, apparently, only moral to kill one to save five when the action is an *indirect consequence* of the intervention.

The first time I was presented with the trolley problem I thought it was pretty dumb. There was something about the inclusion of the 'fat man' that seemed wilfully absurd, almost as if it intended to mock the fallibility of our ethical instincts. I think it betrays an underlying misanthropy that afflicts many people who worship reason. At the time I was enrolled in an Honours degree in Philosophy at Adelaide Uni. Soon after being presented with the trolley problem I dropped out to pursue the even less financially stable option of being an artist. I never got a chance to lay down what I disliked about the trolley problem, so I'll tell you here.

What's wrong with the trolley problem is that it presumes an absolute knowledge of causality that doesn't exist in the real world. The real world doesn't run on tracks. In the real world we never really know what the future holds. We don't know if a fat man will stop a trolley because the real world is infinitely complex. That complexity has forged our ethical instincts over millions of years of evolution, so I don't rush to mock their fallibility.

I liked the way David Walsh went on to suggest that art was a valuable arena for testing those ethical instincts. I started to think about my own posters, but I didn't want to. Instead I came up with my own rebuke to the trolley problem in the form of a silly little allegory called Susan and the Stockman:

> A plane carrying three scientists who have found remedies
> for climate change, cancer and AIDS crashes in the outback.
> They are all critically injured and require organ transplants.
> Complicating matters, their blood type is AB-negative, which
> is very rare.
>
> A stockman finds the crash and calls the nearest hospital.
> They dispatch a surgeon but she's several hours away. The
> stockman must find someone with AB-negative blood and kill
> them to save the world. He checks the pub, the post office
> and the local school without any luck. Time is running out.

He returns to the crash site to tell the scientists he's failed, but on the way he meets a stranger called Susan. The stock-man asks for her blood type. 'AB-negative,' says Susan. He kills her. Delighted, the stockman calls the hospital to tell them the good news. They're overjoyed. Together, they've helped save the world. They advise the stockman to put the organs on ice and await the arrival of the surgeon. 'She'll be there soon,' they say. 'Her name is Susan.'

Perhaps now you understand why I dropped out of my Philosophy course. Why study for three years just to become a more irritating person? After several days of juggling these, and even more annoying questions, Julie and I decided to have a break from Dark Mofo.

We put the afternoon aside for a picnic in the Queens Domain, a hilly area overlooking the River Derwent. We packed some tasty treats and went for a long walk in the bush. I hadn't planned to have a big conversation about our future, but we did.

We'd been together for almost ten years. From the beginning our bond had centred on our shared understanding of each other's creative endeavours. For almost a decade we'd lived in our little blanket-fort of creativity, where the world's expectations couldn't penetrate. Blocking out the rest of the world was a team effort. For a long time neither of us had achieved much. But now that we were finally making progress, we had a growing suspicion that our careers would never become a worthy substitute for the satisfaction of family.

'So the real question is, what do we need to achieve in our careers in order to feel satisfied *enough* that we don't later hate ourselves for starting a family?' I said, in what had started as a romantic chat in the park.

'I don't know,' said Julie. For three and a half years we'd been living in our stinky little apartment in Norwood. There was no future in that place.

'Let's aim for the end of 2018,' she said with some difficulty.

'Do you mean that we can start *trying* at the end of 2018, or do you want to actually have a baby then? Because there's a difference,' I said, trying to keep it playful.

'I mean we can start trying then,' she said in a tone that suggested that I was ruining a perfectly good picnic. I backed off. But as the tranquillity of the setting cleared the air I realised that I needed more.

'Is it because we don't have a house?' I asked.

'That's partly it, but it's also the question of rearranging our priorities,' said Julie. This isn't just another project,' she added. Her choice of words was subtly aimed at me. We both create stuff but I'm the only one who deals in projects. It was a fair criticism. Why should she trust in my ability to support a family? All my time and money goes into producing art projects.

'So let's get a house,' I said.

'You want to buy a house?'

'Why not? Dana and Jess bought a place and they're losers just like us! Do you really want to live in our unit forever?'

'Of course I don't, but …' The silence grew and grew. 'Let's look into it,' she finished eventually.

'So we'll buy a house?' I asked.

'I'm saying we'll look into it!' she said, and I knew this was the best I could hope for. I was happy. We'd made tremendous progress. I promised Julie I wouldn't bring it up again for the rest of the trip. Then I shut up and we enjoyed our rollmops.

The next morning while I was sticking up posters around the

harbour, I found that I had a spring in my step. Since I'd first dropped out of uni and given up on the idea of ever having a stable job and the financial security that goes with it, I'd never allowed myself to believe that I might start a family of my own. I'd always thought that was for everyone else. Only now did I realise that, since meeting Julie, my desire for family had slowly been creeping back. I felt something new in the core of my being where my self-worth was generated. I bounced around the harbour like a little boy. *Was this how Dad felt when Mum was pregnant?* I thought. Julie wasn't even pregnant yet but the mere idea of it had dropped anchor in my mind.

You'll remember that in the first chapter of this book I described my lack of love for the world, the way that I saw the world as worthless and that I preferred not to participate in all its nonsense. I believe it's a feeling that afflicts many people, especially as we cross the threshold from childhood into the adult world. It has something to do with accepting the burden of life's inherent tragedies. For a long time my solution to adulthood was an attitude of detached cynicism. It was an invisible boundary that I built to protect myself from other people's sincerity. Julie was the one who helped me out of that place.

It happened very early in our relationship, when I was still getting to know her family. We were both invited to the wedding of Julie's cousin. We drove three hours north of Adelaide to the small country town of Melrose and arrived just in time to catch the ceremony. We squeezed into the back of the tiny church packed full of family, trapped within its warm embrace. I remember singing and a female priest. I felt uncharacteristically open, and the onslaught of emotion began to break through my defences. Where normally I would be detached, I felt present.

The reception started shortly after the ceremony and the onslaught continued. Speeches revealed layer after layer of heartfelt emotion. Where normally I would snicker and dismiss, now I took it all in. Eventually it become too much. I was watching an old man dancing with a small child when I suddenly stood up, walked out and kept walking. I snaked through the streets of Melrose until I couldn't hear the music behind me. I stopped and realised that I couldn't go back. I just couldn't be in that room anymore without breaking down. I'd had similar experiences once or twice in the past. Normally I'd just escape to a safe place and cry it out, but this time I had nowhere to hide.

Eventually Julie called and gave me the address for our accommodation. I tried to hide the fact that something was wrong, but she wasn't fooled. Later she found me hidden in bed. I was an inconsolable mess, confused and overwhelmed. But when Julie arrived, a question appeared in my mind that made sense of what I was experiencing. I asked Julie if I was good enough. I simply felt unworthy to participate in the abundance of love that flowed through the occasion. Again and again Julie assured me that I was good, that I did belong, and I surrendered to her words. As the boundary between us collapsed, my panic broke into euphoria so powerful that I quickly fell asleep.

I woke early the next morning and the euphoria continued on the drive home. I explained to Julie that I'd never felt that way. It felt like an ecstatic sense of gratitude for absolutely everything, like being on drugs, only clean and guilt-free. Why hadn't someone told me that all this was waiting for me? All I had to do was surrender to love.

There's a good chance you're reading this and thinking, *Silly boy! Everybody knows that love is waiting for all those who surrender their pride.* To that I say, don't be so sure. For every person who is reading this with amused benevolence there is someone else reading this with cynical contempt because, subconsciously, they view themselves as unlovable. It's the kind of pain so overpowering that we hide it from ourselves until it leaks out in hatred or breaks out in violence. For many people it's their default mode of being because they're simply unaware of an alternative. I'm not going to suggest that what happened between Julie and me was as simple as flicking a switch. I fall back into cynicism on a daily basis, but before I met Julie I truly didn't know there was another option.

One of the best things about love is that it doesn't require a rational justification involving trolleys. My silly story about Susan and the stockman could only happen in a world without love. In that sense, love is a necessary counterpart to reason.

As I skipped about Hobart Harbour, I suddenly remembered that John had told me something about love while we were sitting on the wharf in Darwin. *Loving acts are all that matter.* How had I missed that? Then another thought occurred to me: maybe love is what's missing at the core of Keith's worldview. Maybe, without love, the cold scalpel of reason eventually twists around and dissects itself. I wasn't sure how to express that in a poster. Maybe I didn't have to. Maybe it was time that I did a little work on myself before heading out to teach the world another lesson.

Buying In

After the Tasmania mission I returned to Adelaide to discover that my project funds had evaporated. I was relieved. I'd successfully stuck up a few hundred posters and that seemed like enough. I decided to dedicate the rest of the year to making money and buying a house. *My priorities have shifted*, I told myself.

Despite my compulsive saving, I still didn't have enough money for my half of the deposit so I asked my parents for help. They were happy to contribute. I didn't take their generosity lightly. I knew it came with the tacit expectation of providing grandchildren, though they'd never say so explicitly. I tried to let them know that Julie and I were planning to start a family. Even before they gave me the money, I felt I owed them that assurance.

Julie and I found a mortgage broker. We told her that we wanted to buy something well within our means and, after a lengthy process, we were approved for a loan of $300K. I got the impression we could have asked for more but we didn't want to, being terrified enough already. Despite our fear, we found a house and we bought it.

After a few months a sense of belonging set in that was different to living in a rental property. Combined with the prospect of starting a family, it seemed that everything was set for a life of domestic bliss. I started listening to the golden oldies of Cruise FM. My weekends were spent working on the garden. My friends noticed that I seemed 'happier'.

One day, from somewhere within my mind, an ironic thought bubbled up to the surface: *My posters are based on disregarding people's property rights, but now I own property* … It was followed by another thought: *Australia was built on stolen land, but now I own a piece of that land*. What should I do with those thoughts? I didn't know.

In October 2017 Prime Minister Malcolm Turnbull rejected the Uluru Statement from the Heart, which was the key recommendation issued five months earlier at the historic constitutional summit in Central Australia. As I watched Turnbull make his statement, that the proposed idea was neither 'desirable nor capable of winning acceptance', I was reminded of Keith's words. Until then I thought I was ready to stop making posters about Australian identity, but now it occurred to me that I might never stop.

Until then, I hadn't read the Uluru Statement from the Heart. So after watching Turnbull's response I sat down and read the statement in full.

> Our Aboriginal and Torres Strait Islander tribes were the
> first sovereign Nations of the Australian continent and its
> adjacent islands, and possessed it under our own laws and
> customs. This our ancestors did, according to the reckoning
> of our culture, from the Creation, according to the common
> law from 'time immemorial', and according to science more
> than 60,000 years ago.
>
> This sovereignty is *a spiritual notion: the ancestral tie
> between the land, or 'mother nature', and the Aboriginal and
> Torres Strait Islander peoples who were born therefrom, remain
> attached thereto, and must one day return thither to be united
> with our ancestors. This link is the basis of the ownership of the
> soil, or better, of sovereignty.* It has never been ceded or
> extinguished, and co-exists with the sovereignty of the Crown.

How could it be otherwise? That peoples possessed a land for sixty millennia and this sacred link disappears from world history in merely the last two hundred years?

With substantive constitutional change and structural reform, we believe this ancient sovereignty can shine through as a fuller expression of Australia's nationhood.

Proportionally, we are the most incarcerated people on the planet. We are not an innately criminal people. Our children are aliened from their families at unprecedented rates. This cannot be because we have no love for them. And our youth languish in detention in obscene numbers. They should be our hope for the future.

These dimensions of our crisis tell plainly the structural nature of our problem. This is *the torment of our powerlessness*.

We seek constitutional reforms to empower our people and take *a rightful place* in our own country. When we have power over our destiny our children will flourish. They will walk in two worlds and their culture will be a gift to their country.

We call for the establishment of a First Nations Voice enshrined in the Constitution.

Makarrata is the culmination of our agenda: *the coming together after a struggle*. It captures our aspirations for a fair and truthful relationship with the people of Australia and a better future for our children based on justice and self-determination.

We seek a Makarrata Commission to supervise a process of agreement-making between governments and First Nations and truth-telling about our history.

In 1967 we were counted, in 2017 we seek to be heard.
We leave base camp and start our trek across this vast
country. We invite you to walk with us in a movement of the
Australian people for a better future.

In the weeks and months that followed Turnbull's rejection I read all the commentary I could get my hands on. Constitutional reform became my obsession. As an artist, I became fascinated with the mindset of people who believed that the way forward was to alter the fundamental mechanics of Australia's political system. For me, coming from the world of art and culture, it seemed like such an impotent strategy – like watching a team of elephants attempt open-heart surgery on a mouse, using wet spaghetti. There was no lack of intelligence in the discussion, but the legal language conveyed no real feeling. Despite the Statement from the Heart's explicit appeal to emotion, the response from Turnbull and the culture at large seemed comparatively mechanical. The various pundits employed a carousel of legal jargon that was never going to attract broad interest, let alone the support required for a referendum. Over time I lost interest. *If that's the way this game goes, I'd rather not play*, I said to myself, and got back to building my veggie patch.

I picked out a long strip of dirt at the back of our property. There wasn't much growing on it, just a few tufts of scraggly glass, but I could see its potential. In my mind's eye I saw a bounty of vegetables that Julie and I could gift to our neighbours and relatives. I imagined teaching our children how to tend the plants. But as I dug into the dirt I made a nasty discovery – the land was filled with buried rubbish. The property's previous owners had dug holes all over the yard and filled them with household junk and building materials. That's why nothing would grow. I found bricks, rusted metal, plastic children's toys, cutlery, chunks of cement and endless shards of glass. Some of the rubbish pits were shallow but other went down for metres. There was no way of telling from the surface. Once you hit junk you just had to keep digging.

Obviously I'm telling you about the rubbish buried in my backyard because it's a useful metaphor about the inevitability of facing the past. After a couple of weeks of digging up rubbish I gave up on the idea of removing it all. Even after Dad and I had taken trailer-loads to the dump I knew the yard would never be as clean and pure as I had hoped. At least I knew I'd improved it somewhat. With that attitude in mind I read the Uluru Statement again and committed myself to producing a response of my own.

If there's one thing I understand about communication, it's the impossibility of conveying the totality of any desire through a single statement. Given that, it's safe to say that Turnbull didn't really know what he was rejecting. It's also safe to say that the people who wrote the Uluru Statement didn't know what they were asking for, whether it was too much, not enough or the wrong thing altogether. I didn't know either. However, I thought I might be able to understand the fear that motivated its rejection.

What would someone like Keith fear in the Uluru Statement? Surely it was the notion of 'structural reform'. Maybe the prospect of a First Nations Voice was seen as a kind of Trojan horse? After all, what are words like 'sovereignty' and 'self-determination' if not expressions of a latent desire to separate from Australia? If Aboriginal and Torres Strait Islanders went down the road to self-governance, Australia might gradually disintegrate along racial boundaries. Was that a rational fear? To borrow a phrase from the statement itself, 'how could it be otherwise?' Without a real effort to reform Australia's fractured identity, why wouldn't Australia slowly fall apart under the weight of a constitution divided by ethnicity? Regardless, a voting public would be vulnerable to these perceptions, and worse … Maybe that's why Turnbull said it was not 'desirable or capable of winning acceptance'.

It's always been my process to get as close as possible to the people whose opinions I oppose. I think it helps to get inside their heads and surrender completely to their convictions until you can't remember how you got there. Only then, when you're trapped within their worldview, can you start to really feel what they feel. Only then can you attempt to negotiate a way out. I think people like Keith play the world as if it's a game of power while secretly hoping it's not. They toy with the idea that morality's relationship to power is merely ornamental, but they never truly believe it.

As I stood on my little patch of land with my unstable family history behind me and the future prospect of starting a family of my own, I wondered what really holds people together. Surely it's something stronger than the transactional mechanics of legal jargon. Surely it's the power of stories and myths that live inside us and bind us together by the force of shared imagination.

I thought back to the invention of Monga Khan, the Aussie folk hero. Suddenly a new idea occurred to me. What if I tried to reinvent Dupain's Sunbaker? If there is an animating spirit at the core of people like Keith and Turnbull, what would that spirit think and feel?

AWAKE!
The Sunbaker is dreaming the Australian dream
He's dreaming of atonement
He's dreaming of forgiveness
He's tired from all he's taken

What colour will his skin be

Whose head will appear on his coins

What shape will his flag be

When the Sunbaker awakes?

I designed this poster at the end of 2017. At the time it was as close as I could come to making a poster about love. I think people like Keith still believe in love but they hide it from themselves. They hide it in symbols like the Sunbaker, or the national anthem or the Australian flag, because those symbols are powerful enough to protect their love. Art has the ability to reshape those symbols and unlock the love therein so that individuals, families, tribes and nations can be reborn and awaken anew. I know that sounds a little grandiose, but that's what I believe. I'm an artist; it's my job to believe in the redemptive power of art.

At the time I made this poster I thought it was for Keith, but really it's for my brother Julian. I don't know how to explain that in a logical way. I just remember the feeling of trying to design something personal and that this is the way it came out. By the end of 2017 there was a feeling growing inside me that was quite different to anything that had motivated my previous projects. It was more of a personal longing. It didn't feel like strength. It felt like vulnerability. I thought it might go away. I wanted it to go away. I wanted to block it out with another attention-grabbing project. So I cooked up some more attention-grabbing posters and tried one more time to outrun my own demons.

Please Be Offensive

At the beginning of 2018 I went through my annual phase of doubting whether I was really an artist. I had little confidence in my 'AWAKE!' design. *Too many words*, I told myself. Why would anyone share a poster that takes time to read and offers no clear solution? It had none of the punch of my previous designs, so I put it to one side and tried to forget about Australian identity.

Luckily there was plenty of other noise to focus on. After one year of Trump in the White House, the global culture was busy servicing the appetites of a new generation of outrage junkies. *Why not?* I thought. *Why not jump into that vortex and see where it takes me?*

There were so many battlegrounds to choose from. I could go into race, gender, immigration, free speech, economic inequality, climate change, gun control, the rise of the far right or the rise of the far left. Via YouTube and Twitter I could easily discover who the thought leaders were. If debate got bogged down in nuance I could float downstream to where the debate stayed simple, punchy and entertaining. I could rapidly internalise the swirling mass of rhetoric and regurgitate it as my own. Maybe I'd start small with a few funny memes. Gradually I'd build my following into a baying mob of supporters whom I could deploy against easy prey. I noticed that the landscape was quickly filling up with backyard pundits competing for the prize of 'most provocative player'. How could I make my brand stand out? What if I was never truly an artist? What if I was just another political entrepreneur?

The only indication that I might still be an artist was the fact that the entire spectacle made me feel sick. Everyone expressed the same disgust, yet everyone remained committed to a system of social media that thrived on polarisation. All the old optimism of a 'democratised' media landscape had evaporated. Instead it seemed that democracy itself had become suspect.

Something about the term 'political entrepreneur' was still interesting to me, so I decided to make it my new theme. Until then I'd been unabashedly left wing. However, from an entrepreneurial perspective, declaring my allegiance to just one side seemed like a dumb move. Wasn't I alienating half the political market? What if I made some right-wing posters? So I did.

We're only truly equal in death, so there's a bitter irony in the fact that whenever we try to enact *total* equality it always seems to end up in a big pile of skulls. To me this seemed a very dark statement, but many people saw it as completely innocuous, simply because it bore the word 'equality'. Such is the unimpeachable power of that particular platitude.

At first I was disheartened by the poster's superficially warm reception until I received a message of support from a Cambodian refugee, who interpreted the skulls as victims of the Khmer Rouge. *If she got it but the normies didn't, all the better*, I thought.

Now that I had a right-wing poster, I needed a new left-wing poster to balance things out. I decided to turn my focus to the United States. Julie and I were planning to travel to America later in the year. It was to be our last hurrah before we committed ourselves to a life of parental servitude. At some point I realised that the perfect issue for an Australian street artist in America would be gun control.

Following the Las Vegas shooting in October 2017 and the Parkland shooting in February 2018, the debate over gun control had reached fever pitch. Several comedians, including one Australian, had already made careers for themselves by boasting about the success of Australia's gun laws. The fact that a conservative Australian government had introduced the restrictions made the point all the more irritating to American conservatives. I felt confident my poster would trigger their annoyance.

Finally, I needed a third design to pull it all together and draw out the sour taste of irony. I wanted to make a spectacle of my naked capitalistic impulses. I wanted to celebrate the sheer nihilism of America's political entrepreneurship and pour my fuel upon the fire.

Please Be Offensive

Whenever you make an offensive comment you are creating jobs in the outrage economy and helping to distract an entire generation from the realities of adulthood.

Thankyou.

I waited until the fourth of July to launch my project amid the drunken fragility of American patriotism. It worked. Unsurprisingly, the gun control poster attracted the most attention. It was the easiest to read and the most topical. My inbox quickly filled with American rage – some vile, some quite funny. But I got the impression that most people understood the project as an act of satire. The people I engaged with often revealed the playfulness of their game, confirming my core suspicion: our culture of outrage is little more than a profitable sport.

I attracted similar outrage from people on the left. It was strange being called 'alt-right' and a 'socialist leftard' on the same day. Departing from past practice, I was letting the audience decide which posters I would stick up. For every poster sold I promised to stick up ten posters on the streets of America. In this way the audience would effectively control my agenda. Many people chose 'Equality' and 'Please Be Offensive', but most chose the gun control poster, so I guess I'm still a lefty. However, I couldn't deny the project's overall nihilism in its attempt to exploit both sides of the political dialectic.

In previous years I'd committed to my posters with a frenzied intoxication that fed upon my personal attachment to Australian identity. Now I couldn't muster the same enthusiasm. So what if America's political discourse was munted? But nor could I rest on that sentiment. How can someone with plans to start a family afford to be so cynical? Surely my host country of America deserved something more than my empty jibes? Surely the oldest democracy in the world deserved a little more respect?

With that sentiment in mind I designed four new posters.

Out of many possible affirmations, I deliberately chose the seemingly antiquated notion of brotherhood and sisterhood. I actually liked their theological tone. Despite being an atheist since I was nine years old, I was gaining more and more respect for the power of religious metaphors. I often wonder whether our regressive tribalism is a result of our failure to find a secular substitute for the way religion universalises our familial bonds.

I felt sure my new posters would provide a potent catalyst for my experience on the streets of America. However, in the back of my mind I could hear a faint voice telling me that America was just a distraction. I knew it was true. I was just running away from my problems by creating a spectacle. I'd soon discover that the last thing America needed was another spectacle.

America

On our first morning in Los Angeles, Julie and I went down to Venice Beach to take in the sprawling kaleidoscopic extravaganza of American freedom in all its lurid intensity. It was eight a.m. on a Sunday and the place was crawling with exhibitionists 'living their best life'. In a way it was beautiful, maybe even inspiring ... Then I saw this guy.

He wasn't joking. Online it's hard to tell whether anyone is really sincere but on the street it becomes obvious pretty quickly. I rushed over to the man in the picture, whom everyone else was ignoring, and asked for an explanation. As I held up my phone to make a video he was happy to share his thoughts.

'You can't measure the curves, can't measure the spin ... Water is flat, man, water is a level. You can use a level with the bubble in it because water is inside, because water finds a level,' he told me as he pointed at the horizon of the Pacific Ocean. 'The only reason they say it curves is because of gravity.'

He let me take his photo, then off he went to spread the word. Sadly, I didn't get a chance to follow up on his claim that 'Space is fake'. Apart from his sign, nothing about his appearance indicated insanity. He probably had a good job. He seemed quite peaceful, like an everyday American pursuing his hobby. I guess in America you're free to be crazy as long as you're not hurting anyone.

Early the next morning I got to work spreading my own theories. Julie and I were living among the hipsters of Silver Lake. As I followed Sunset Boulevard towards Hollywood I found plenty of spots to place my posters. I encountered almost no resistance.

'You Aussie?' asked an elderly man as I was sticking up a gun control poster. He had ridden up on a bicycle that was customised to resemble a prop from *Mad Max*. He was wearing a mixture of denim and piercings over skin that had turned to leather in the sun.

'Yep, I'm an Australian,' I said, continuing my work.

'You can't change the Second Amendment,' he said flatly, through a cloud of facial hair.

'Yeah, I know. I like your First Amendment though,' I said, then shifted the conversation towards his bike. I was happy to avoid a debate and he was happy to chat about his bike and his love of Los Angeles. No matter how disconnected some people seemed, especially in LA where everyone was acting out a fantasy version of themselves, a deep civic pride shone through. Several times I was told off, or granted approval, by homeless people who insisted on having their say over my posters being stuck up near their spot. That never happens in Australia.

'Take care, brother,' they'd say. Sometimes it would be 'God bless you.'

I divided my efforts between West Hollywood, the Sunset Strip, Echo Park and Downtown. The following week I was in San Francisco, where I made a special trip out to Berkeley to make my little contribution to America's epicentre of progressive thought. On the university campus I found myself walking among the hubbub of orientation week. Fresh young students collected handfuls of fliers at the festival of stalls advertising their clubs to potential new members. Everything from archery to Zahanat, the all-male fusion dance group, was on offer. Nobody seemed to pay much attention to me putting up my posters. I was just part of the circus.

The following week I was sticking up posters in Brooklyn to a similar lack of interest. Being a street artist in the hipster capital of the world couldn't be more passé. Many of the best graffiti artists had formed companies that painted commission murals for brands like Evian and Louis Vuitton. Covered in anti-graffiti protective coating, these giant ads dominated the streetscape. Many warehouses that once housed artist collectives had recently been demolished to make room for high-rise luxury apartments filled with young professionals. They all worked across the river in Manhattan. Every morning they clogged the subway like a swarm of talking haircuts, leaving their

toddlers in the care of immigrant nannies who clustered together to gossip in the park.

Eventually I took my last twenty posters to Times Square and gave them away. It was near midnight and the place was packed. I was relieved to see the last few posters disappear into the crowd.

Afterwards I stood and gawked at a group of black Israelites pouring racist bile upon confused tourists. Behind them a glowing billboard of Beyoncé and Jay Z completed the picture of America, the land of absurd contrasts.

The next day I went to Brooklyn's Bushwick Inlet Park to look across the East River at Manhattan and try to make sense of my trip. A week before, Julie and I had been in Yosemite, among the Sierra Nevada mountains. But now, as I looked upon the sprawling mass of humanity that is the New York City skyline, I was surprised to admit that I found it more impressive than Yosemite. It looked like a vast engine of human imagination, inviting me to dive into its furnace. If I were younger I'd have happily submitted to its promise of transformation, but now I felt like I had too much to lose. I had plenty waiting for me back home.

I have one last poster to show you. I designed it just before leaving for America. The idea came to me on a whim, maybe due to my general dissatisfaction with the rest of my posters. When I shared the new design it was immediately popular, which made me curious. A few people hated the design, which made me even more curious. They wanted to know whether I was trying to be ironic, which of course I was, but not in the way they were hoping.

In truth, the new design was an experiment and I wanted to be its guinea pig. When I got back from America the experiment would begin. It was time to go home and take some responsibility for my real problems, the ones that were right in front of me.

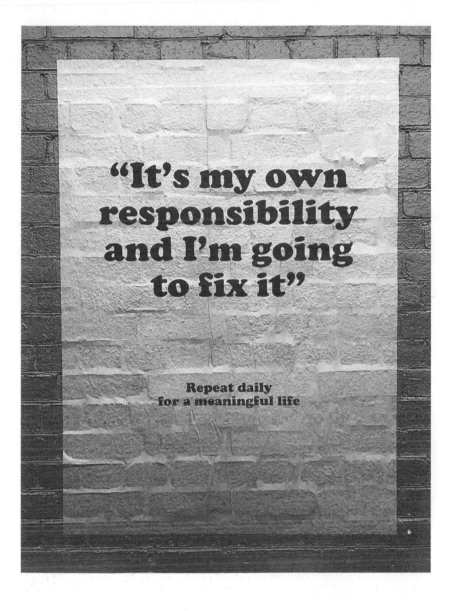

Getting It Done

The week after we got back from America, Dad came over to help me move some screens. He's always driven a bigger car than mine and I still rely on his help moving things. These days his body is getting old and I need to do the heavy lifting, otherwise he'll gladly hurt himself 'getting it done'. I lifted the screens over the roof rack and Dad threw straps across the top. We each tied a clove hitch before adding octopus straps for tension. The ceremony was complete in under a minute with barely a word spoken.

When I was a kid I'd watch Dad work on the house. I could stand there for hours, holding tight to the possibility that I might be called upon to hand him a tool at a crucial moment. That enthusiasm dried up in my teenage years, and only came back when I realised I still needed him. By the time I moved out of Tooth & Nail Studio, I had a chance to do some building of my own. Dad and I took two months to build a 6x6 metre shed that would have taken professionals two days to construct. We lost our tempers with each other more times than I can count, but we got it done.

The screens on the roof were headed for a printer on the other side of town who'd offered to expose my new designs. We had a forty-minute drive ahead of us. As we drove along in silence my head was swimming with technical problems. Had I stripped the screens correctly? Where the transparencies opaque enough? Were the designs any good? That was the real problem. I started running through my catalogue of imaginary arguments with all the people who would hate them.

'How's Julian?' I asked out of nowhere.

'The same,' said Dad, after a pause.

I'd seen Julian less and less since he'd come to zippole two and a half years earlier. Even when I did visit the house, which wasn't often, he rarely showed his face. Dad and I didn't talk about him, so it was like he didn't exist. It was easier that way. But on that day I wasn't in an easy mood. I felt like attacking any problem within reach.

'What's the plan?' I said.

'What do you mean?' Dad replied.

'Well, Julian's a 36-year-old man who's been living with his parents for well over a decade. He doesn't have a job. He doesn't seem to want a job. All he seems to do is troll the internet. That's the problem, so what's the plan?'

'I don't know,' said Dad quietly.

'Have you tried talking to him about it?' I asked.

'He won't listen to me.'

'Why not?'

'Oh, I don't know!' said Dad.

A couple of times in the past I'd confronted Dad about the situation with Julian and it always got stuck at this point. I'd encourage Dad to sit down with Mum and hash out a plan. Maybe they could give Julian an ultimatum? Maybe they could ask him what he needed from them? Maybe Dad could find a support group of parents who have the same problem? Maybe he could try *something*? Anything would be better than ignoring the problem for another year. But every time I tried to push Dad into action he'd placate me with agreement and then nothing would change. I never bothered to talk to Mum. She was in complete denial.

We slipped back into silence. I knew how the conversation would play out if I pushed it any further. What was the point? Besides, I had my own life. What did I care if there was a black hole at the centre of my family, crushing them slowly?

But I'd been thinking about it for years. I'd been projecting my family's problems onto Australia for years. Of course I cared. It wasn't for lack of caring that I failed to confront the matter. It was cowardice.

'Why won't Julian listen to you?' I asked again.

'I don't know!'

'I think you do,' I said.

We had twenty minutes left on our drive. If I didn't push the point now, it would be another year before we spoke about it again. I didn't want to speak about it again. I wanted to get it done.

'It was fifteen years ago that we drove to Canberra to get Julian,' I said. 'He managed to live there, on his own, for two whole years. So there's really nothing wrong with him. He can take care of himself.'

'Yes,' said Dad.

'So don't you think that he's just feeling humiliated? Don't you think it might help him if he felt forgiven for his failings? Don't you think you could help him get over that humiliation?'

'He *won't* listen to me,' Dad insisted.

'You can't think of any reason why Julian doesn't trust you?' I asked. 'Was it always like that between him and you? Even when he was little, he wouldn't listen to you?'

'I don't know,' he said.

Now I was getting pissed off. Now I was sure he was playing dumb. Now I was sure I wanted to hear him say it.

'I think you do know,' I said. 'I think you can probably think of a pretty good reason why Julian wouldn't trust you.'

There was a long pause. In that moment I knew his secret was right on his mind. I wondered how many times over the past thirty-two years he'd been this close to telling the truth. Moments came to mind. Lost opportunities. I wasn't going to lose this one.

'Did something happen between you and Mum when we were little?'

'Yes,' said Dad.

And like that, it was gone. The secret was broken. The invisible boundary had been crossed. I knew it would all come out. I felt dizzy.

'When you boys were very little I fooled around on your mum. It was a completely stupid thing to do and I've regretted it ever since. Mum and I decided to never tell you boys.'

'How old was Julian when it happened?'

'Four.'

'Do you think he remembers?'

'I'm not sure,' said Dad.

We pulled up in front of the printers. Dad started to get out of the car but I asked him to wait.

'Did Mum forgive you?' I asked.

'Well, she said she did, but the way I saw it, that shame was just something I should learn to live with. We decided to never, *ever* tell you boys because we didn't want you to think that you weren't wanted. Your mum had to carry that secret too, so why should I feel forgiven?'

'I'm thirty-five years old, Dad. I've been around long enough to know that nobody's perfect. I've had moments of weakness. Everyone needs to be forgiven. But if you keep going around carrying this shame, how can you forgive Julian?'

Dad nodded. Then he looked at me and said, 'Okay, let's get on with it.'

So we got out of the car and untied the straps. The next day I started writing this book.

A Real Boy

My initial fear in writing this book was that the scale of my story would not match the grandeur of the theme. I was afraid that adultery plus posters would not equal a tale of spiritual poverty. Is my story big enough? Are my posters clever enough? Am I good enough? It's all the same question, really. It's all the same fear. Give in to that fear and it's amazing how quickly the world can fall apart. But we rarely give in completely. We mostly just diminish ourselves in little ways. We commit little sins of neglect, often disguised as modesty. We tell ourselves that it doesn't really matter, but it all adds up. Before you know it, there's a pile of sins so large that you need to write a book just to make sense of it all.

You'll notice that I never asked my dad to apologise. I don't feel that I'm owed an apology. I forgive him regardless. My dad's already given me more than I could possibly ask for and he's suffered too. I'm no better than he is. I've made mistakes and I count myself lucky that they haven't been big ones. If anything, I've learnt from his mistakes. If I hadn't known about our family history, maybe I would have ruined my own marriage a long time ago. Who knows? The one thing I do feel that I am owed is the truth. I think everyone deserves to hear the truth. I have faith in the truth. I believe in its regenerative qualities. The truth reverberates and heals in unpredictable ways.

One thing I haven't said yet is that I'm grateful to my mum. I'm grateful for her cunning and tenacity in keeping our family together. If she hadn't undermined my dad's affair he might never have returned. Sure, they could have done a better job at forgiving one another, but I think they did the best they could with the skills they inherited. The fact that my parents stayed together out of duty to me and my brothers is ultimately humbling. The fact that they used shame to hold us together is the obstacle they now need to overcome. They should do it for the sake of my brothers but also for themselves. I believe they can, because I believe they're still in love.

My obsession with Australian identity grew out of my family dysfunction, but to what extent is a nation like a family? A nation is composed of love as well as power. Nations are born; they grow and die. Nations protect, and they oppress. Above all, nations, like families, are composed of stories.

But if my experience can be boiled down to one essential lesson, it's that nothing can move forward without truth-telling. If lies persist, they gradually erode love into shame. If Australia is to survive, it needs to take full responsibility for its past. Occasionally, every one of us entertains the idea that a truth kept hidden can be undone by its un-telling. It cannot. Left untold, the truth is only delayed in the force it *must* manifest in the world. So best not keep truth waiting, best not give truth reason to be vengeful in its arrival. Best pay the truth its due, lest it turn to spite and fury.

I recently caught up with my younger brother, Simon. For the past three years he's been renovating his apartment between bouts of depression. Dad's done most of the work. The apartment is starting to look really good and he should be able to move in by the time this book comes out. He sees a psychiatrist every week and he's getting better. I spoke to him about his drinking at Christmas and he admitted that he blacked out and vomited in his room. We laughed about it but he knows it's a problem. When we spoke about Julian, Simon suggested that he should get some regular help from a mental health professional. It's not a bad idea but first my parents need to admit there's a problem.

Recently I told my parents that I was writing this book. They were a little defensive at first, but once I assured them that it was written in good faith and with the intention of clearing the air, both were supportive. They expressed concern for how this book might affect my brothers, especially Julian. I'm also concerned about that, but I'm more concerned it might not affect him at all. I hope that he can hear my message: that I love him and that he need not feel ashamed.

My parents asked whether I'd include a particular story. I had already written it down but was unsure about including it. The fact that my parents brought it up, out of the blue, was enough to convince me that I should share it with you. So here it is …

In my first year of high school I got in a fight with a bully named Ben Dell. That fight would define my future in ways I still haven't resolved. Actually, we had two fights.

The first happened at recess on a Wednesday. My friends and I were playing handball near the library when Ben kicked our ball away. Chris Marinos got in Ben's face and I jumped to Chris's defence. Ben tried to hit me but I just kept blocking his shots and landing punches of my own. Suddenly someone yelled 'Teacher!' and the fight was over. Ben totally started it and I totally won. Surely I'd never hear from Ben Dell again.

The problem was that we were nerds and Ben couldn't handle the humiliation of losing to a nerd. My friends and I hung around the library because that was the lowest-status patch in the whole school. We were trying to hide. I can't imagine why Ben had even walked near us unless he was visiting the library to borrow a book titled *Smashing Nerds: A Beginner's Guide.*

The next day I started to hear subtle rumours, like: 'Oi Drew, Ben Dell's going to smash you tomorrow at lunch. You're fuckin' dead!' The fact that the whole school seemed to relish the prospect of seeing me 'smashed' left me feeling a little deflated. Although I wasn't surprised; even at age thirteen I was an arrogant kid – but not so arrogant that I wasn't afraid.

That night at the dinner table I told Dad about the upcoming fight. Dad turned to Julian and said, 'You take care of your little brother.'

The next day a crowd of a hundred kids had gathered around the library when I arrived for lunch. Ben swaggered up and started getting in my face. 'I don't want to fight,' I said, so Ben pushed me. I pushed Ben, so Ben punched me hard in the face. It was as hard as a prepubescent boy can punch, but not as hard as a kick to the head, which is what I gave Ben. He crumpled. Just as I was about to cement my victory in front of the entire school and elevate my status above the rung of 'arrogant nerd', someone shoved me to one side. It was Julian.

Ben was slightly bigger than me but Julian was *much* bigger than Ben. He didn't stand a chance. Julian pulled Ben's jumper over his head and started raining down blows. I immediately felt sorry for Ben, who cowered into a ball. Then, as my brother stood over his quivering victim, he proclaimed to the wincing audience the words that would go down in family lore as the epitome of righteous victory: 'Don't mess with the family!'

A moment later the teachers arrived, but Julian and his mates had disappeared. I got detention. Ben never bothered me again. On the one hand it wasn't a bad result. For the next year nobody came near me. But later they did. I learnt to never tell my family when I was being picked on. From then on I dealt with the bullies myself.

Obviously, part of me wishes I'd dealt with Ben myself, but that's not the point of the story. It's really a story about Julian. The reason my parents brought it up is because Julian is still proud of it. He's happy that he helped me because that's the closest we came to showing affection towards one another. I was vulnerable and he helped me. Now he is the vulnerable one and I wish I could help him. But Julian is too proud to ever admit weakness, let alone surrender to love.

One of Julian's favourite quotes comes from the psychologist Abraham Maslow: 'I suppose it is tempting, if the only tool you have is a hammer, to treat everything as if it were a nail.' But Julian's version is even better. He says, 'When you're holding a hammer, everything *looks like* a nail,' implying that your very perceptions are dictated by your abilities. When we lack the tools to heal we go looking for things to hate, because it's less painful than hating ourselves. The fact that Julian seems to understand that much about our predicament only demonstrates the difference between knowing the path and actually walking it.

Ultimately I don't believe that the wrongs of the past can ever be audited to perfection. There is no such thing as an immaculate history – not for individuals or families, or for nations. But I do believe in slow and humble progress. I believe that every one of us needs to be forgiven, and we long to enact that need through art, culture and ceremony. With the courage of truth and love, who knows what potential we might manifest? I hope we never stop growing up.

Ten Rules for Great Propaganda

For those of you who have read this book because you're interested in political art but not necessarily in my family history, I offer my sincerest apologies. The fact you've read this far is truly admirable. In fact, you've been so patient that you deserve a treat! So here are my ten rules for great propaganda. I hope you find them useful in overcoming your appetite for political art.

Raise a question, not a statement

Admittedly, 'Real Australians Say Welcome' is not a great example of this approach. By asking a question you engage the audience in discussion rather than conflict. That's a good place to start.

Be clear

Every artist hides in ambiguity. Admit that you want to be understood by attempting to be understandable. You don't need to squeeze the entire universe into every artwork. At least make the question clear. The answer can be as ambiguous as you like.

Empathise with your enemy

Try to understand the people you oppose because they're not really your enemy – they're actually you with a different worldview. What is it that they're really trying to protect? Maybe you can show them another way to protect it.

Flatter your enemy

Appeal to their strengths. Like it or not, the world actually needs conservative people. Show your enemy that you admire their strengths and they'll be more willing to admit their weaknesses.

Negotiate

What are you willing to forgo in order to get what you want? Until you have an answer to this question you're not ready to negotiate, so why should the other side negotiate with you?

Irritate both extremes

Try to pull your audience towards the centre by irritating people at both extremes of an issue. Unless you're being attacked in equal measure by the extremists on both sides, you're doing something wrong.

Be an adult, not a utopian

Humans are not perfectible; only children and utopians think otherwise. Don't believe me? Try perfecting yourself and see how far you get. By acknowledging your own faults you'll discover empathy for everyone else's.

Create myths

You're not a scientist, or a historian or a dentist. You're an artist, so do what only artists can do and create myths. Myths have a dynamic power unlike anything else because they are inherently imaginative. Myths are open to interpretation. They invite the audience to adapt and reimagine the story as they see fit. Above all, myths invite the audience to embody values in ways that histories cannot. That's what makes myths *live* in the world.

Surrender to love

Love is more than an ornamental compensation for the Faustian bargain between innocence and power. Love is the essential circuit-breaker. Without love you're just another powerbroker, so believe in love.

Use the street

The street is the oldest forum we have. It is the place between places. Art on the street assumes no authority beyond the value of voice over property. Therefore, don't be surprised if your art gets vandalised in turn. Just remember, there's always another wall.

Acknowledgements

Thanks to Anna Goldsworthy for pointing me in the right direction at a moment when this book might have come to naught. Thanks also to Chris Feik and Jo Rosenberg for always making me feel that I was in safe hands. Finally, thanks to my wife, Julie, for gently reminding me, about twice a year, that I needed to write a book. If I ever write another one it'll be about Julie and what being with her has taught me about the relationship between love and creativity.

Image Credits

All images copyright © Peter Drew except for the following:

Pages 23, 24, 25 and 26: artwork copyright © Ali Reza Muhammad

Page 36: photograph copyright © Ali Morad

Page 41: artwork copyright © as follows:

> Top row: left © Nathan Nankervis, centre © Marc Martin, right © Evie Barrow

> Middle row: left © Sara Dickins and Alana Waterson, Poppies for Grace, centre © Neryl Walker, right © Julia Busuttil Nishimura

> Bottom row: left © Kitiya Palaskas, centre © Alice Lindstrom, right © Rachelle Blake

Page 95: out of copyright; image courtesy of the National Archives of Australia

Page 97: out of copyright; image courtesy of the National Archives of Australia. NAA: D596, 1909/687

Page 98: out of copyright; image courtesy of the National Archives of Australia. NAA: MT19/4, 1916/MONGA KHAN

Page 100: artwork copyright © Jake Holmes

Page 118: still from *Monga* copyright © Manal Younus

Page 131: artwork copyright © Andrea Smith

Page 132 top: artwork copyright © Paul Kisselev

Page 132: bottom: artwork copyright © Gabriel Cunnett

Page 142: photograph copyright © Harjit Singh

Page 143 and 146: photographs copyright © Daniel Pockett

Pages 156 and 157: out of copyright; photographs courtesy of the National Archives of Australia. NAA: D596, 1928/10702

Pages 160 and 161: photographs copyright © Jessica Clark

Pages 182, 219 and 231: photographs copyright © Julie White